Fortress • 58

Vietnam Firebases 1965–73

American and Australian Forces

Randy E M Foster · Illustrated by Peter Dennis

Series editors Marcus Cowper and Nikolai Bogdanovic

First published in 2007 by Osprey Publishing
Midland House, West Way, Botley, Oxford OX2 0PH, UK
443 Park Avenue South, New York, NY 10016, USA
E-mail: info@ospreypublishing.com

ISBN 978 1 84603 103 8

Cartography by Map Studio, Romsey, UK
Mono line drawings by Peter Dennis
Design: Ken Vail Graphic Design, Cambridge, UK
Typeset in Monotype Gill Sans and ITC Stone Serif
Index by Alan Thatcher
Originated by United Graphics, Singapore
Printed in China through Bookbuilders

08 09 10 11 12   11 10 9 8 7 6 5 4 3 2

A CIP catalog record for this book is available from the British Library.

FOR A CATALOG OF ALL BOOKS PUBLISHED BY OSPREY MILITARY AND AVIATION
PLEASE CONTACT:

Osprey Direct, c/o Random House Distribution Center, 400 Hahn Road,
Westminster, MD 21157
Email: info@ospreydirect.com

Osprey Direct UK, P.O. Box 140, Wellingborough, Northants, NN8 2FA, UK
E-mail: info@ospreydirect.co.uk

www.ospreypublishing.com

Acknowledgments

I am very grateful to everyone who helped me develop this book,
directly or indirectly. From the USA, notably James R. Arnold and
Roberta Wiener, of Lexington, Virginia, have my fullest possible
thanks for conducting the essential photo research in the US
National Archives, which provide the major part of the images
used in this volume. Don Aird, formerly with Charley Battery
1/83rd Field Artillery, was also of enormous help. Peter G. Tsouras,
Lt Col, US Army Reserve (ret) and Brig Gen David T Zabecki,
editor of *Vietnam* magazine, both also provided significant
inspiration. From Australia, Bill Houston was generous with
his time and expertise, as were RSM Christopher Jobson and
Lt Col Greg McCauley (both gunners). From the UK, I am very
grateful to Peter Dennis, Gary Hardwick, the publisher Tony Bird
and the historians John Ellis, Ed Flint, Andrew Grainger, Professor
Christopher Duffy, Drs Paddy Griffith and Paul Harris, as well as
the late Drs David Chandler and John Pimlott.

Artist's note

Readers may care to note that the original paintings from which
the color plates in this book were prepared are available for
private sale. All reproduction copyright whatsoever is retained
by the Publishers. All enquiries should be addressed to:

Peter Dennis
Fieldhead
The Park
Mansfield
NOTTS
NG18 2AT
email: magie.h@ntlworldcom

The Publishers regret that they can enter into no correspondence
upon this matter.

The Fortress Study Group (FSG)

The object of the FSG is to advance the education of the public
in the study of all aspects of fortifications and their armaments,
especially works constructed to mount or resist artillery. The FSG
holds an annual conference in September over a long weekend
with visits and evening lectures, an annual tour abroad lasting
about eight days, and an annual Members' Day.
The FSG journal *FORT* is published annually, and its newsletter
Casemate is published three times a year. Membership is
international. For further details, please contact:

The Secretary, c/o 6 Lanark Place, London W9 1BS, UK

Contents

Introduction

The place of fortification in a widening war

For a number of years before 1965 the USA maintained a clandestine army, which grew to over 20,000 troops in South Vietnam, under the name of "military advisers." Their aim was to boost the military skills of the Army of the Republic of Vietnam (ARVN), although they often became frustrated when their advice was misunderstood, skewed or simply ignored. In operational terms this was a time when the Viet Cong (VC) was inexorably growing in power as the authority of the South Vietnamese government crumbled. In terms of fortification it was a time when ARVN installations were protected by a bewildering collection of different and often haphazard arrangements, ranging from forts and pillboxes built by the French before they departed in 1954, to lightly defended "strategic hamlets" built under President Diem in an ill-conceived attempt to ape British methods in Malaya. From 1961 US Special Forces (USSF) were also building their own chain of camps in remote areas where the montagnards could be protected and organized.[1] In this period there were many examples of ARVN positions being overrun by night-time assault or more peacefully infiltrated and subverted by VC sympathizers. The logistic infrastructure was not well developed, so not only were specialized building materials in short supply, but there were few large fortified main base facilities outside the capital area around Saigon.

All this changed in 1965, when the deteriorating security situation led President Lyndon B. Johnson to commit mainforce US ground units to the struggle, with a landing by the 9th Marine Expeditionary Brigade at Da Nang on March 8. Ten US and four Allied (mainly from the Republic of Korea, Australia and New Zealand, Thailand and the Philippines) divisions (or division equivalents) would follow during the next four years. They would provide significant reinforcements to the beleaguered ARVN garrisons, and largely put an end to the habit of losing defended positions. Against this, however, the American deployment was also the signal for a massive increase in military support for the VC from the regular North Vietnamese Army (NVA), which in turn led to mainforce battles on a scale not seen since Dien Bien Phu in 1954. The war was visibly escalating on a monthly basis, as both sides fed in more troops and strove to provide them with ever-greater levels of munitions and logistic supplies.

The Americans faced a particularly serious logistical problem, since before 1965 South Vietnam had few ports and airfields. This, incidentally, helps explain why so many of the air operations were based in Thailand, or on aircraft carriers, or, in the case of the B52s of the Strategic Air Command, as far away as Guam. Even then, a major new port had to be built inside Vietnam, at Cam Ranh Bay, with smaller ones at Qui Nhon and Nha Trang; as well as many new airstrips, both large and small. Through these facilities would flow weapons, ammunition, aircraft, vehicles, fuel, equipment, building materials and every other conceivable type of item in unimaginable quantities –

A soldier of Battery C, 1st Bn, 82d Arty Regiment, relaxing with his music outside a poorly fortified, timber-framed hut in March 1969. The roof offers protection against the rain, but little else. The ammo boxes filled with earth or laterite offer cover from direct fire or shrapnel only up to waist height, so one hopes there is a proper foxhole somewhere nearby. (US National Archives)

---

[1] See Gordon L. Rottman's analysis in Osprey Fortress 33: *Special Forces Camps in Vietnam 1961–70.*

even though, before Cam Ranh was opened, the transport ships often had to wait to be unloaded in the limited Saigon docks for longer than they had taken to sail the 10,000 miles from California. The US deployment could never be as rapid as the escalating military situation demanded; and ironically it would peak at over 600,000 men (and 4,000 helicopters) only in 1968, just as the political decision was being taken to pull out of the country – a four-year delay, almost as long as it had taken to fight the entire First World War. Thus although the arrival of troops and *matériel* was eventually truly awesome in scale, it never seemed to keep up with the voracious demands of the ever-expanding war, and in one perspective it might even be described as "lacksadaisical and short of urgency."

Nor did this consideration apply only to the arrival of the major mainforce formations: it also slowed down many of the less obvious but still totally fundamental details, such as the arrival of village-building materials for the local counter-insurgency war, or the arrival of armored fighting vehicles (AFVs) for the mainforce war. In 1965 there had been a general assumption, based on a reading of French defeats in 1953–54, that the helicopter should be used for the majority of tactical transportation in Vietnam, rather than ground vehicles. This analysis would have far-reaching implications for American fighting methods, since it imposed a marked delay in shipping and deploying anything that could not be lifted by a helicopter. Towed versions of the 105mm and 155mm howitzers were preferred to the self-propelled (SP) versions, and neither tanks nor armored personnel carriers (APCs) began to arrive in large numbers until about 1967. This was partly due to the sea-lift problems mentioned above, although it may also be attributed to a certain technological futurism attaching to the brand new airmobile concept.

For whatever reason, it was only in 1967 that the Americans finally discovered that modern armor could actually operate very well not only on the roads to which the French had been restricted, but also over some 65 percent of the countryside. Even in the wet season tanks could still move over 46 percent of

45th ARVN Artillery Regiment digging bunkers and trenches on commanding ground at FSB Mike Smith, 1970. Note the use of tree trunks in the constructions. This is yet another example of the way in which building materials had to be improvised and scrounged, since there were never enough ready-made construction elements provided from central stores. (US National Archives)

FSPB Thrust

In a communication to the author, RSM Christopher Jobson of the Royal Australian Artillery described FSPB Thrust, which was built in March 1969 beween the coast and Dat Do in Phuoc Tuy province:

An example of an FSPB established by I ATF in South Vietnam was "Thrust", which was made-up of one field artillery battery (six 105mm howitzers), an infantry battalion headquarters (HQ), an infantry support compony-minus (consisting of a company HQ, two mortar sections [four 81mm mortars], an anti-amour platoon [eight 106mm recoilless rifles] and an assault pioneer platoon, along with a signals platoon-minus).

The Base also housed elements of an infantry administrative company, which included the Regimental Aid Post, and an infantry rifle platoon. For added protection the Base also had two troops of APCs, with each troop consisting of 12 carriers armed with .50 calibre machine guns. The perimeter also housed two LZs, one for a Medium Lift Helicopter (50 metres in diameter) and the other for a Light Observation Helicopter (37 metres). The total area occupied by "Thrust" was approximately 800 x 700 metres.

According to Michael P. Kelley (*Where We Were in Vietnam*, pp. 505–06) "Thrust" was built on sand, which reflected light upwards into the garrison's eyes. It included a sandbagged 40ft tower for a night observation device (NOD), which was a more powerful version of a Starlight Scope. This tower was nicknamed "the leaning tower of Pisa."

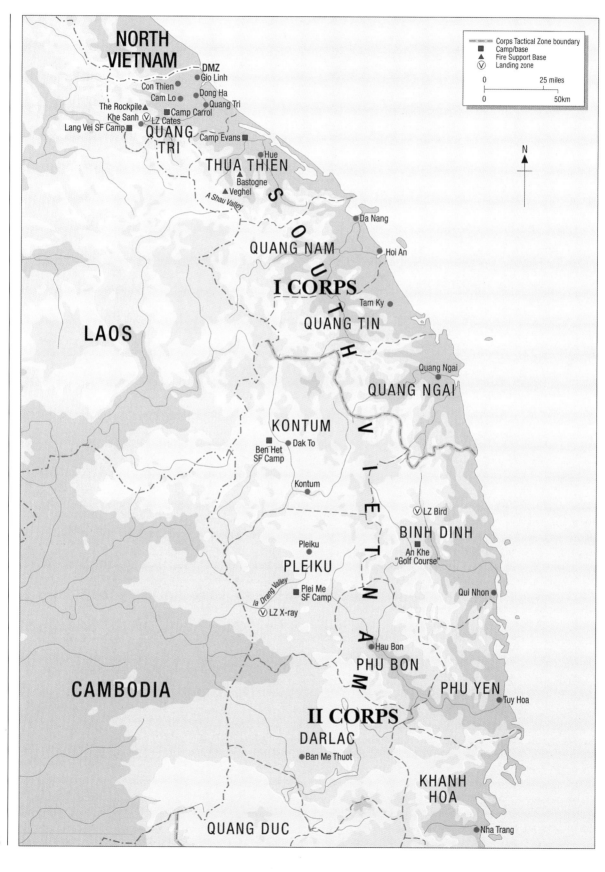

NORTH VIETNAM

Corps Tactical Zone boundary
■ Camp/base
▲ Fire Support Base
ⓥ Landing zone

0 _____ 25 miles
0 _____ 50km

DMZ
● Gio Linh
● Con Thien
Cam Lo ●
● Dong Ha
Camp Carrol
● Quang Tri
The Rockpile ▲
Khe Sanh ● ⓥ LZ Cates
Lang Vei SF Camp ■
QUANG TRI
Camp Evans ■

● Hue
THUA THIEN
▲ Bastogne
▲ Veghel
A Shau Valley

N

● Da Nang

SOUTH

QUANG NAM
● Hoi An

I CORPS

Tam Ky ●
QUANG TIN

LAOS

QUANG NGAI
● Quang Ngai

KONTUM
Ben Het ● Dak To
SF Camp

● Kontum

VIETNAM

ⓥ LZ Bird

BINH DINH
An Khe
"Golf Course" ■

Pleiku ●
PLEIKU
Ia Drang Valley
Plei Me ■
SF Camp
ⓥ LZ X-ray

Qui Nhon ●

● Hau Bon
PHU BON

PHU YEN
Tuy Hoa ●

CAMBODIA

II CORPS
DARLAC
● Ban Me Thuot

KHANH
HOA

QUANG DUC
● Nha Trang

6

South Vietnam, and APCs over very much more. And if the armor could open the way, soft-skinned motor transport could often follow. The helicopter turned out to be slightly less revolutionary than its more evangelical disciples had liked to imagine, as Gen Don Starry was delighted to explain in his excellent book *Mounted Combat in Vietnam*. After 1967 the resurgence of armor would be of growing importance in every year the war continued, as US and ARVN operations that had previously been airborne increasingly went back to using roads. Meanwhile the NVA was also gradually increasing its own use of armor, building up from the PT-76 assault on the Lang Vei Special Forces camp in 1968 until its T-54 main battle tanks finally rolled into central Saigon in April 1975.

A war in five acts

The Second Indochina War may be seen as a tragedy in five acts:

Act one, 1957–64: the gradual "slice by slice" defeat of the ARVN by the VC, despite the presence of a growing number of US military advisers.

Act two, 1965–67: the slow deployment of US mainforce formations and their firebases, which was met by a rather greater deployment of the NVA into South Vietnam. The ARVN was relegated to local counter-insurgency against the VC in "the village war," but it was significantly underfunded in the interest of the high-profile (and high-cost) US maneuvers against the NVA. The Ia Drang battle was fought in November 1965, followed by a series of large-scale operations, such as *Masher-White Wing* in Binh Dinh province, January–March 1966; *Cedar Falls* in the Iron Triangle, January 1967, and *Junction City* in Tay Ninh province, February 1967.

A Sikorsky CH-54 Sky Crane picking up equipment from a gun position at FSB Challenge (Binh Dinh province), April 1970. When it was first deployed in 1966 the Sky Crane was the most powerful heavy lift helicopter in the Army's inventory, capable of carrying a payload of 20,000 lb., although its performance was soon overtaken by later marks of the considerably more numerous CH-47 Chinook. The curious shape of the Sky Crane is explained by its capacity to hitch a variety of carrying pods, containers or vans flush with the central structural beam; for example a Conex box, accommodation for up to 87 troops, or a surgical suite. (US National Archives)

OPPOSITE PAGE I and II Corps Tactical Zones.

A CH-47 Chinook lifts off from FSB Challenge (Binh Dinh province), carrying an M102 105mm howitzer, April 1970 (Battery A, 4th Bn, 42d Artillery). Note the wire mesh anti-rocket screens. The "A" version of the Chinook in Vietnam could carry an external payload of 16,000 lb., but the later "C" version could take well over 22,000 lb. The M102 howitzer weighed something like 3,500 lb., while the older and heavier A101A1 version had weighed almost 6,000 lb. Thus in both cases a Chinook could carry the gun crew and plenty of ammunition as well as the piece itself. (US National Archives)

Act three, 1968: the US deployment reached its peak, as both combat techniques and logistic arrangements were perfected. However, the fighting also rose to a crescendo in the Tet Offensive early in the year, with additional enemy attacks continuing into the summer. The NVA siege of Khe Sanh ran from January to April. Although the Tet fighting effectively destroyed the VC, it also destroyed confidence in the USA that the war was winnable. President Lyndon B. Johnson recognized that his Vietnam policy had failed, and announced he would not stand for reelection.

Act four, 1968–73: President Nixon was elected on a policy of US withdrawal, covered by the following: (a) continuing US operations at key points (for example, Hamburger Hill in the A Shau Valley, Thua Thien province, May 1969), although these would decrease in scale and intensity as units were pulled out, and some of those that were left became affected by loss of motivation. (b) The "Vietnamization" of the war.[2] (c) Ground offensives into Cambodia, May 1970, and Laos, February to March 1971. Despite their successes, these operations failed to prevent a major NVA assault on the South at Easter 1972. This offensive tested Vietnamization to the limit; but the ARVN held firm and demonstrated that Nixon's policy could indeed be successful. Then (d) there were two major US bombing offensives during 1972; these persuaded the North Vietnamese government to sign a treaty that generously allowed the Americans to get out of the South. Note that almost half of all US casualties were suffered in the 1968–73 period, during which withdrawal had already been decided.

Act five, 1973–75: war between the NVA and the ARVN continued but, as a result of the Watergate scandal, Congress soon cut off most of the aid to the ARVN upon which "Vietnamization" had been based. The major NVA offensive of 1975 (using conventional warfare rather than guerrilla tactics) was therefore decisive. Saigon fell at the end of April and Vietnam was at long last reunified.

---

[2] The process of handing over the main burden of the war to the ARVN.

Defending the bases

Obviously the more combat formations that were deployed in-country, the more bases they would require. They needed safe places where they could store their munitions; maintain their aircraft and vehicles; rest, command and administrate their troops; and heal their sick or wounded. This was doubly true since the scale of issue of advanced weaponry was normally far greater for the Americans than for the ARVN, at least until the policy of "Vietnamization" was introduced from 1968 onwards. The American way of war also demanded a much higher rate of fire and expenditure of ordnance, as well as relatively lavish rear-echelon facilities. Hence logistic requirements and the "tail to teeth" ratio were both exceptionally high. At its peak of 600,000 men in-country, the US were operating only 10 divisions, which averages the staggering and unprecedented total of 60,000 men per "divisional slice." Admittedly a proportion of them was assigned to supporting the ARVN and other allies; but on the other hand, it must be remembered that vast numbers of extra personnel were concurrently employed on the line of communication all the way back through San Diego, CA to Marietta, GA and Detroit, MI. Regardless of how these statistics may be assessed, the fact remains that on average only about one in ten of the in-country US soldiers and helicopters were available for combat operations at any given time. This left them with only a few (if any) more troops on the ground than the enemy could deploy; and even then, out of that number most of the Americans would still be assigned to defensive rather than offensive tasks, while most of the enemy were not.

When he reached Camp Bearcat (a US main base at Long Thanh near Long Binh) in May 1968, the Australian soldier John Goodwin was amazed at the lavish scale of the facilities he encountered:

> When we arrived, it was like driving into a major city. The Yanks had all the mod cons; swimming pools, putt-putt golf, tennis courts, clubs with poker machines and draught beer – whatever you wanted. We enjoyed their hospitality, plenty of beer. As a little sideline, I met a Yank sergeant who worked in the morgue of the 9th Division, and he ... (treated) us to pizzas which he kept on trays on a slab in the morgue. A little morbid, but just a thing that happened.[3]

From left to right: a captured Soviet 122mm DKB rocket launcher and two mortars (Soviet 82mm PM37 [Chinese Type 53] and Soviet 120mm HM43 [Chinese Type 55]) on display in April 1971 at Phu Bai or Camp Eagle, just southeast of Hue. In an attack on a firebase all three of these weapons would contribute to an intense initial bombardment designed to surprise the Freeworld troops in the open, at the same time as signaling the start of the action. (Don Aird)

[3] McAulay, Lex *The Battle of Coral – Fire Support Bases Coral & Balmoral, May 1968*, p.61.

From left to right: a captured Soviet Degtyarev 12.7mm (.51-cal.) DShK38/46 (Chinese Type 54) AA machine gun; a Goryunov 7.62mm "heavy" (actually medium) machine gun (Chinese Type 57); and a Chinese 75mm Type 56 recoilless rifle (copy of US M20). As with all communist weapons used in Vietnam, the basic designs were manufactured in both the USSR and China, with slight differences in each case. The machine guns, especially the 12.7mm, were the weapons normally posing the most serious threat to Freeworld helicopter pilots when they flew near the ground in bandit country. (Don Aird)

All this implied that an exceptionally high proportion of the US effort in Vietnam had to be allocated to static installations, which then had to be defended. A whole new network of fortified positions was created, which in both quantity and quality quickly outstripped the earlier French and ARVN (and even the USSF) efforts. Camp Bearcat itself, for example, had started life as a French airfield, and then served merely as a USSF camp until it was greatly developed into a fully fledged divisional base from December 1966, used variously by the US 9th Division and by the Royal Thai Division. It was named after the radio callsign of the Special Forces unit that had been stationed there in the early 1960s; by 1968 its whole character and scope had expanded enormously. By contrast the 1st Cavalry Division (Airmobile)'s huge Camp Radcliffe main base at An Khe (better known as "the Golf Course" because it was left with grass rather than being bulldozed down to the bare soil), was cut out of the brush on a site (over 1km long) that had never before been fortified. It was selected because it was near Qui Nhon, where the division initially came ashore in September 1965 – although at that time no port facilities had yet been built there. Before the An Khe base and its communications with Qui Nhon could be opened, a brigade of the 101st Airborne Division first had to conduct Operation *Highland*, comprising no less than eight airmobile assaults and a series of ground attacks, in which the number of enemy killed was put at 692.

The new US defenses always had great tactical strength; but the general problem of manpower overstretch nevertheless persisted. Each Freeworld main base, combat base or forward operating base (FOB) needed at least a brigade of

Two captured NVA 122mm rockets put to ornamental use at the front gate of a firebase near Phu Bai. They could deliver a powerful explosive charge in a bombardment. (Don Aird)

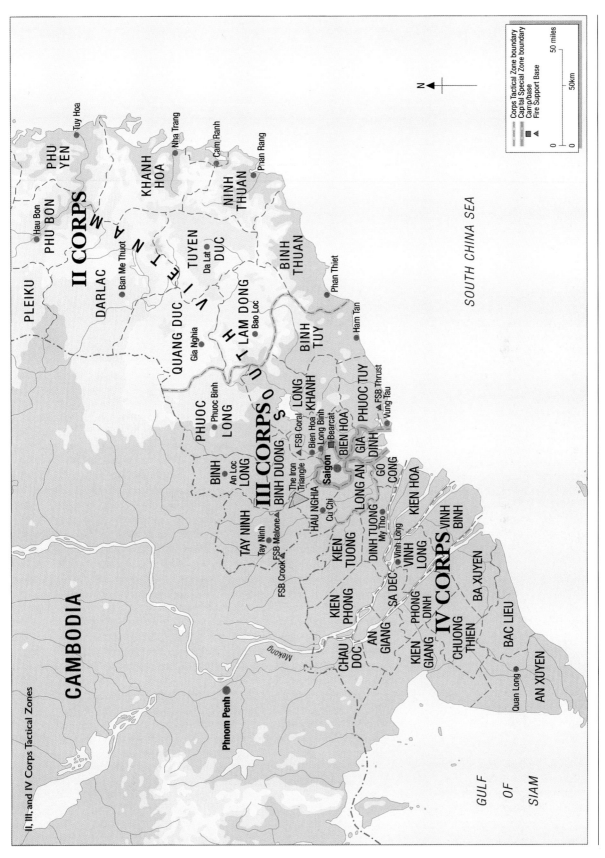

II, III, and IV Corps Tactical Zones

CAMBODIA

Phnom Penh

GULF
OF
SIAM

SOUTH CHINA SEA

II CORPS

PLEIKU

DARLAC

PHU BON

PHU
YEN

Tuy Hoa

Hau Bon

Ban Me Thuot

KHANH
HOA

Nha Trang

Cam Ranh

NINH
THUAN

Phan Rang

TUYEN
DUC

Da Lat

LAM DONG

Bao Loc

BINH
THUAN

Phan Thiet

QUANG DUC

Gia Nghia

PHUOC
LONG

Phuoc Binh

BINH
LONG

An Loc

TAY NINH

Tay Ninh

FSB Crook

FSB Malone

BINH DUONG

The Iron
Triangle

HAU NGHIA

Cu Chi

FSB Coral

Bien Hoa

Long Binh

Bearcat

BIEN HOA

LONG
KHANH

GIA
DINH

Saigon

LONG AN

GO
CONG

PHUOC TUY

FSB Thrust

Vung Tau

BINH
TUY

Ham Tan

III CORPS

KIEN
TUONG

DINH TUONG

My Tho

Vinh Long

KIEN
PHONG

CHAU
DOC

AN
GIANG

SA DEC

VINH
LONG

PHONG
DINH

VINH
BINH

KIEN
GIANG

CHUONG
THIEN

BA XUYEN

IV CORPS

KIEN HOA

BAC LIEU

Quan Long

AN XUYEN

Mekong

N

Corps Tactical Zone boundary
Capital Special Zone boundary
Camp/base
Fire Support Base

0   50 miles
0   50km

A perimeter guard from 42d Artillery Regiment looks out into the boonies from the high ground at FSB Challenge (4th Division area, II CTZ, Binh Dinh province). He has a tripod-mounted .5-cal. machine gun and is protected by sandbags and a wire mesh rocket screen. (US National Archives)

troops to defend it, and would cover many acres of land, including all the facilities that would normally be found in a peacetime garrison – ranging from the post exchange store (PX) to the typing pool, from the laundry to the lorry park, and from filing clerks to filling stations. Normally, as in the Marines' Khe Sanh combat base in 1968, the whole thing would be built around an airstrip, either large or small, for fixed-wing aircraft.[4] Yet of course neither fixed- nor rotary-wing aircraft could operate safely if the enemy was able easily to bring down fire on the center of their operating base; so there was always an incentive to expand the major defended perimeters and conduct active patrolling outside them, to prevent the enemy siting his weapons anywhere within range.

Thus the majority of Freeworld troops found themselves pinned down in defensive or support roles at any given time, rather than being free to conduct "search and destroy" or other truly mobile missions. In these circumstances it could be said that the static installations were very much the "typical" scenes of military life in Vietnam, for most Freeworld forces, for most of the time. For that reason, if for no other, they are well worth study. Yet there is another even more significant reason; despite a very few well-publicized failures, the awesome defensive strength of these fortifications added up to a massive military success – one of several that somehow failed to impress the general public back home. Once a particular site in Vietnam had been fortified, even if it was no more than a temporary company-sized firebase, it became to all intents and purposes invulnerable to any attack that the VC or NVA could mount – although doubtless it might not have been able to resist for more than 10 minutes against a fully equipped Soviet motor rifle regiment. Fortunately for the Americans, their "state of the art" in defensive warfare had advanced sufficiently far by the 1960s for them to be able to beat off any number of Vietnamese foot infantry, even if they were supported by plentiful mortars, rockets and rocket-propelled grenades (RPGs). By contrast we must also mention that in the 1960s the US "state of the art" in offensive warfare was still dramatically far short of the condition it

---

[4] For all aspects of the Khe Sanh battles, see Gordon L. Rottman's account in Osprey Campaign 150: *Khe Sanh 1967–68*.

has reached today, some 40 years later. Therefore, although the defense of US firebases in Vietnam was definitely a great success in tactical terms, the offensive operations that were launched from them could often be a great deal more problematical.

The perimeter of a large port or airfield complex, or of a fighting division's main base, represented a vastly larger type of fortification than a temporary artillery position of one battery and one infantry company, which might be set up by helicopter airlift and then removed by the same means a week or two later. The latter might perhaps sometimes accommodate a few ground vehicles, especially armored ones; but usually it would rely for its logistics on one or two landing pads for helicopters. Equally, a permanent USSF camp, set up to accom-

Members of the 4th Infantry Division unloading simple digging tools, and a dog, from a Huey, at FSB Challenge (Binh Dinh province), 1970. (US National Archives)

modate a battalion-sized force of montagnard CIDG and their families, would be a radically different type of installation from a temporary battalion-sized US tactical base designed to launch search and destroy sweeps into the surrounding countryside, as part of a major mainforce battle. Apart from anything else, the former might perhaps boast only two artillery pieces if it was lucky, whereas the latter might sometimes be allocated a whole regiment of three batteries. In the case of the (mostly Australian) FSPB Coral in May 1968, which did indeed enjoy this level of provision, it could also call upon the fire of no less than 41 US batteries firing from other bases in the area, in calibers ranging from 105mm to 8in. (i.e. 203mm), not to mention massive airpower on call, even including B52 "Arclight" strikes. This is a mobilization of firepower far more reminiscent of the two World Wars than of the sort of small-unit, counter-guerrilla patrolling that had been the norm in many parts of Vietnam during most of the 10 years before 1965, and in some parts of the country long after that.

CH-47 Chinook transport helicopters at FSB Bastogne, Thua Thien province, April 16, 1968. The red clay soil was characteristic of much of Vietnam, as was the generally "untended" bare earth appearance of most firebases. The mighty Chinook was introduced into the Army's inventory in 1961, and is still going strong to this day. (US National Archives)

What is a firebase?

In this book we will not be discussing either main base areas or Special Forces camps, but only the "firebases" used in the mainforce war fought by the USA and her allies. So the question immediately arises: just exactly what do we mean by a "firebase"? Clearly it had to be capable of delivering fire, and this usually implied artillery rather than merely mortars, recoilless rifles or small arms. The artillery was very often the driving force in the whole design and construction of firebases, so it will be central to our concerns in this volume. In theory each firebase was supposed to form part of an interlocking grid of artillery sites that would allow shells to be brought down anywhere within the territory. Even if it was on its own, out on a limb, the firebase would still be designed to give artillery support to infantry patrolling in the area within range of its guns, and in fact infantry would not normally be expected to operate without artillery on call. As Gen David Ewing Ott explained in his essential book on field artillery (*Field Artillery, 1954–73*, p.55), "Only on rare occasions did manoeuvre forces in Vietnam operate beyond the range of friendly artillery."

The range of a 105mm howitzer was a little over 11,000m, while that of a 155mm howitzer was 14,600m. These ranges represented the radius around each firebase within which sustained, high-volume fire could be laid down. Hence if two FSBs were 22,000m apart with 105mm howitzers, or 29,200m apart with 155mms, they could engage any enemy located in the whole of the ground between them. Then again, the 8in. SP howitzer was very accurate to 17,000m, while the range of a 175mm SP gun was a staggering 33,000m, which theoretically enabled FSBs to be 66km apart – although this gun could not be fired as rapidly or as accurately as the lighter howitzers, and was normally used only to reinforce a group of firebases containing the latter, from afar.

"Charley's Worry" – an SP M110 8in. howitzer at FSB Sally (Long Khanh province, III CTZ), March 1970. This was the most accurate weapon in the artillery inventory, with a maximum range of 17,000m. The same chassis was also used for the longer-range but less accurate M107 175mm gun, and the two tubes could be interchanged in the field. Note the layout of the hard standing and the defensive berm. (Don Aird)

The site of Camp Carroll, Quang Tri province, in 2005, looking northwest toward a modern white concrete monument, which can be seen on the far side of a grey concrete bunker from the late 1960s (this may have been an ops room or protected store). In 1968 long-range 175mm fire was delivered from here in support of Khe Sanh and its relief operation, *Pegasus*. But as with most other firebase sites, there is very little to be seen today of the extensive field fortifications built during the war. (Ed Flint and Paul Harris)

If we attempt to be very much more specific than the idea that "firebases were supposed to deliver fire," we quickly find ourselves in deep waters, since there appear to be so many alternative and interchangeable definitions of a "firebase" that no firm generalizations can be made. Many sites were commonly referred to in many different ways, even when their designation was not officially changed. Almost any defensive position was likely to be called a "firebase" of one sort or another, sooner or later; but then again it was probably even more likely to be called a "landing zone" (LZ), provided a helicopter ever landed in or near it. In this war, of course, helicopters were a major means of transport, so almost every firebase was very likely to be an LZ as well. Then again, infantry patrols might be

Sign outside the FDC (below ground with overhead cover) at FSB Navel (or Naval) Binh Dinh province, April 1970. The slogan aptly sums up what a firebase was all about. This particular one is armed with M102 105mm howitzers. (US National Archives)

sent out from any base, regardless of its size, so any base might justly be termed a "patrol base." By the same token, any base could also be called a "camp," so there really can be no certainty. Table 1 sets out one possible set of definitions, although all of them were always very flexible. Not only did normal usage tend to ignore the finer points as laid down in military manuals, but the manuals themselves also varied widely from one division's area to another's.

Table 1: some different names for defensive positions	
Main base or "base camp"	A large and permanent fortified area with a full airfield.
Combat base, forward operating base (FOB), or permanent LZ	Smaller than a main base, but still a major permanent fortification, often including an airstrip.
Fire support base (FSB)[1]	Smaller than an FOB and also usually fairly permanent; but with LZs for helicopters rather than fixed-wings.
Special Forces camp or Civilian Irregular Defense Group (CIDG) camp	Similar to an FSB. Usually garrisoned by a USSF "A" team and a battalion of montagnards with their families.
French fort	A small, permanently fortified (normally triangular) camp left behind by the French. Sometimes allegedly poorly planned for defense in the conditions of the 1960s, which of course were not those of 1946–54.
Fire support patrol base (FSPB), patrol base or forward fire support base (FFSB)[1]	An FSB (with which it was often confused) built for just one operation, hence not as permanent, elaborate or as deeply dug in as a more formal FSB.
Landing zone (LZ)	Anywhere used for landing helicopters (and in theory fixed-wing aircraft too; but the term was normally used just for helicopters). The majority by far were temporary and entirely unfortified, but there would always be one or more LZs inside all of the above types of fortification, apart perhaps from those dating from the French era.
"Strategic hamlet"	In theory a relatively lightly fortified hamlet, manned and controlled by local militia on the pattern used successfully in Malaya; but in practice they were often left unbuilt and very far from controlled areas (in Vietnam a "hamlet" was often a discrete segment of a "village," which might sprawl over many kilometers).
Night defensive position (NDP)	A position occupied by infantry for just one night, with only the barest minimum of fortification.

Notes

The above names were often interchangeable, and there was certainly no standardization of the size of the garrison, or the duration of occupancy, in any given case. Sometimes the same site was officially reclassified once or more during its lifetime.

[1]   These are the two types that will receive most attention in this book.

At any given moment a very large number of FSBs and FSPBs could be found in South Vietnam – and from 1970 there were also a few just outside it: first in the Cambodian border area and then, in the following year, in Laos. In his essential and monumental book *Where We Were in Vietnam,* Michael P. Kelley listed something upward of 8,000 different sites altogether during the period 1945–75, although maybe only one or two thousand of them may have been active at any one time. Even so, it cannot be stressed enough that such an effort was still very costly in terms of manpower, and even at the peak of the US deployment in 1968 there were never enough troops to go round. Even if the firebases were 22,000m apart, an unfeasibly large number of them would have

Unloading shells into an improvised magazine at FSB Anzio (Thua Thien province), January 1969 (Kentucky National Guard, Battery B, 2d Bn, 138th Artillery). The shells are big but the soldiers are also relatively small! A 105mm shell weighed 33 lb. (excluding cartridge case); a 155mm weighed 95 lb.; and an 8in. weighed 200 lb. Both of the last two used bagged propellant. (US National Archives)

been needed to cover the whole of South Vietnam, which was around 1,000km long and 150km wide. The Freeworld forces therefore had to concentrate their operations, and their firebases, on certain selected areas at any given time. In theory it was hoped that once a particular area had been cleared of the enemy it would remain clear, although in practice this was far from always the case.

Inserting a fuse in front of a wooden-framed ammunition bunker in a gun position, June 1969. "WP" marks the compartment for White Phosphorus rounds. Each gun position would have a series of compartments: one for each different type of shell. (US National Archives)

A patrol sets out from a firebase

Building a firebase

The first thing that had to happen in the building of a firebase was that someone had to take the decision to build it. Initially this would be the tactical commander of some particular mobile operation, who would be following a more general directive from a higher authority. In the Ia Drang campaign of November 1965, for example, Gen William C. Westmoreland, commander of Military Assistance Command, Vietnam (MACV), assigned Maj Gen Harry W. O. Kinnard to use his 1st Cavalry Division (Airmobile) to clear the area southwest of Pleiku of NVA. Kinnard in turn assigned different tasks to each of his brigades, with the main battle from November 9 being run by Col Thomas W. Brown's 3d Brigade. Out of that brigade it was 1st Battalion of 7th Cavalry, commanded by Lt Col Harold G. Moore, that was given the key job of reconnoitering and securing LZ "X-Ray" in enemy territory at the foot of the Chu Pong mountain. It was there that a ferocious battle was fought from November 14 to 16 – the biggest of this first year of major US deployment. The site had been chosen partly because it was in a clearing where 8–10 Huey helicopters could land at a time, and partly because it was close to the area where a battle was desired. There were thought to be no enemy in the immediate vicinity; but even so the LZ was fully "prepped" by air power and artillery fire before ground troops were landed to secure it. Once the troops were on the ground they were quickly able to dig in to a standard sufficient to beat off repeated attacks by more than an entire fresh NVA regiment, although at times it would be a close-run thing. Despite heavy incoming fire, it was nevertheless found to be possible to continue landing reinforcements and supplies by helicopter, and to evacuate the casualties. Within two days the LZ had been converted into an "instant firebase."

"Peace Maker" – truck-mounted quad .5-cal. AA guns, for use in the ground defense role. These guns had a terrific rate of fire and a very heavy punch, even though normally only two guns would fire at any time. FSB Veghel was built on two linked peaks atop a steep hill, 27km southwest of Hue, in Thua Thien province. It had been captured from an NVA battalion by 1/327 US Infantry in April 1968 after a very bloody three-day fight. It was recaptured from the ARVN by the NVA in the Easter offensive of 1972. (Don Aird)

OPPOSITE **A patrol sets out from a firebase**
Not all the operations mounted from a firebase would be airmobile. Increasingly as the war went on there was a return to armored fighting vehicles, since they could carry much heavier firepower than was possible with helicopter-delivered light infantry. It was found that far more of South Vietnam was accessible to tanks than had previously been thought; but even more was accessible to APCs. Shown here is an up-gunned M113 armored cavalry assault vehicle (ACAV), which turned out to possess the optimum combination of firepower and mobility for supporting foot soldiers.

Preliminary reconnaissance was nevertheless of enormous importance, and the helicopter commanders had to be involved at every stage, as much as the commanders of the troops to be landed. The routes to fly in and out of the LZ had to be selected, and if possible they each had to be different, to maintain the maximum element of surprise. The most normal flying formation was a "V" with the point towards the target and each helicopter stacked a little higher than the one in front, to avoid the rotor wash. Upon arrival at the LZ the whole formation would ideally set down simultaneously, so it was necessary to know in advance, through reconnaissance, exactly where each ship was intended to go.

Reconnaissance was also important for structural as well as tactical reasons. The right type of terrain had to be chosen, to fit the intended purpose of the firebase. Large parts of Vietnam were covered not only in jungle but also in hills or mountains, and both those factors posed multiple questions to the would-be firebase designer. Was there a good field of fire around the perimeter, or would the jungle have to be cleared? Was it desirable to occupy a flat open field where multiple helicopters could land, or was the idea to "take the high ground" and seize narrow mountain peaks from which the surrounding countryside could be commanded? Was the type of soil suitable for embedding the artillery pieces? Was there a source of water on the site? Were there civilians living in the area, or could it be considered a "free fire zone"? How rapidly was the site expected to be fortified? And how long was it expected to continue in use? How far away from logistic support would it be, and on what scale could it be provided? Robert J. Nicoli, operations officer in 3d Engineer Battalion, serving in I Corps Tactical Zone (CTZ) in 1968–69, noted:

Over the past 8 months, the 3d Engineer Battalion has found that on those occasions when engineering difficulties or problems arise during the constructions of a FSB, those problems can almost always be attributed to the fact that the engineer commander has not been afforded the opportunity to conduct a visual recon.

At LZ X-Ray in 1965 the US troops had gone in with their eyes open, after Lt Col Moore had conducted a close-in reconnaissance from the air, and then landed with the leading troops. By contrast at the Australian FSPB Coral on May 12, 1968 the key commanders were shown the terrain from a helicopter

Battery A, 8th and 4th Artillery, at USMC Combat Base Elliott (Quang Tri province, near the Rockpile), firing 175mm guns, July 20, 1969. The area of the Rockpile gained fame precisely for the long-range 175mm fire that it could bring down in support of the Khe Sanh combat base, which was some 22km to the west-southwest. The Rockpile itself was an inaccessible jagged crag, but the larger Combat Base Elliott was on flatter ground. Judging by this photograph it seems to have enjoyed some especially neatly built fortifications. (US National Archives)

The Rockpile. In 1968 this was a dramatically steep and high USMC observation and re-broadcasting center commanding the whole area of Khe Sanh. It could be supplied only by helicopter, although at its foot (to the south) Combat Base Elliott was built, on the site from which this photo was taken in 2005. (Ed Flint and Paul Harris)

on the day before the attack; but the pilot would descend no lower than about 4,500ft (almost a mile high) for fear of enemy fire.[5] This made a key difference to the outcome, since from that height it was impossible to see that the selected LZs were covered in saplings up to 3m high, which would have to be cleared before helicopters could ever hope to land. It was only the next morning, just 10 minutes before the leading troops were due to land, that the ghastly truth dawned. All timings had to be set back while other troops were sent in overland to cut down the saplings, with the result that when the landings did finally take place they were pretty chaotic. Many of the troops were disoriented and lacked adequate time to dig in before dusk, and they failed to establish a complete perimeter. Just as with LZ X-Ray three years earlier, there were a number of enemy regiments in the area; but at the poorly reconnoitered FSPB Coral they were able to do a great deal more damage to the future firebase before it could be properly set up and finally made impregnable – which it nevertheless eventually was.

According to Philip Caputo's famous saying, "Happiness is a cold LZ" – or in other words a place where there was no incoming fire during the crucial two minutes while a helicopter was landed. A central point in the initial reconnaissance of any LZ was to discover whether the enemy was present on the selected site. This was best done by troops on foot or in armored vehicles, who would not have to suffer the uncertainties and hazards of a helicopter insertion. In practice, however, it was rarely possible to provide them unless there were already plentiful friendly forces close at hand on the ground. From the time of the Tet Offensive onwards there was admittedly a growing understanding that armor had a greater role to play than had previously been imagined, so increasing efforts were made to co-ordinate it with airborne operations. Nevertheless it was far more normal for the reconnaissance to be conducted by air observation, both visually and from photographs. If there was any doubt about the enemy presence near the planned LZ, there would also be a "reconnaissance by fire" to flush out anyone who might be lurking in the immediate vicinity. This in turn would merge into the "prep fires" immediately preceding and accompanying the landing, to give it covering fire and keep the enemy's heads down in the crucial moments when the helicopters were sitting ducks. One disadvantage sometimes noticed was that too much prepping would excessively churn up and mangle the trees and undergrowth on the LZ and its surrounding area, making it more difficult to clear the site later. Nevertheless the nervousness attending any air assault tended to encourage maximum prep fires rather than restrict them.

---

[5] The maximum altitude to which a 12.7mm [.5-cal] machine gun could reach was 5,000ft, whereas an AK-47 rifle could manage only about 1,000ft.

1 Command and communication bunker
2 Occupied gunpit
3 Chinook landing 155mm howitzer
4 Medical bunker
5 Central gunpit, ready to receive gun/ammo
6 Gunpit under construction
7 FDC bunker
8 Perimeter trench with bunkers
9 Wire barriers
10 Cleared field of fire

Set drills and procedures for air assaults were worked out early in the war, at least as early as the Ia Drang battle of November 1965. Specialized teams of helicopters would be assembled for the many different tasks:

- OH-6A or OH-58A light observation helicopters and Command UH-I Hueys for the initial reconnaissance and to help acquire targets.
- Light fire teams for air-to-ground bombardment (each of two gunships, or one gunship and one light observation helicopter; the gunships were all Hueys up to September 1967, but thereafter were increasingly replaced by AH-1G Cobras), possibly supplemented by Hueys acting as aerial rocket artilley (ARA).
- Blue teams to carry the infantry (each of five transport Hueys, capable of carrying in eight men each, or a whole platoon of 40 men between them).
- CH-47 Chinooks and possibly even CH-54 Sky Cranes to bring in artillery, heavy supplies, or any other cargo – in some operations including civilians and their buffaloes.
- Command Hueys for continuing coordination and radio communications.
- Last, but by no means least in the minds of the troops, the medical evacuation "Dustoff" Hueys: the vital reassurance that wounded soldiers would probably not die.
- Artillery and fixed-wing aircraft would also be co-ordinated into the initial bombardment and then remain on call to protect the site and its surrounding terrain in case of need. The fixed-wing aircraft would be directed by a forward air controller (FAC) flying in a light airplane such as an O-1 Bird Dog.

The US Marine Corps used a different mix of helicopters – and commanded their own fixed-wing airforce – but essentially their air assaults followed a similar pattern. Instead of UH-1 Hueys they had H-34 Choctaws and CH-46 Sea Knights, both capable of carrying two squads of soldiers rather than one. Instead of Chinooks they had various versions of the Sikorsky "Jolly Green Giant," which, like the Chinook, could carry a whole platoon – but faster.

As part of an air assault there would usually be a notional timetable for the occupation of the site; not only in the reconnaissance and insertion phases, but throughout its subsequent life and eventual evacuation.

In the event, taken over the war as a whole, far more LZs turned out to be "cold" rather than "hot." However, if a major battle was already raging in the area, it would become almost inevitable to encounter incoming fire. In Operation *Lam*

Remains of a Claymore mine, photographed in 2005 close to the site of Plei Me Special Forces camp (Pleiku province), which featured in the Ia Drang campaign in late 1965. Given scrap scavenging at other sites, together with their being covered by rubber, coffee or pepper plantations, this is one of the few sites where one gets any sense of it having been involved in the war, because a few artifacts can still be found, and the lines of sight around the base remain largely intact. (Ed Flint and Paul Harris)

Table 2: phases in the life of a firebase

1. Reconnaissance and planning by all authorities involved in the operation (air/helicopter, infantry, artillery, engineers).
2. Prep fires from air and/or artillery based in other firebases.
3. Insertion: air assault or, occasionally, insertion overland.
4. Initial hasty fortification (including getting the CP underground quickly).
5. Reinforcement: bringing in extra troops, artillery and heavier stores, including a bulldozer.
6. More serious fortification, consolidation and clearing the site and the glacis. Digging a perimeter trench, installing wire barriers, sensors etc.
7. Possible offensive operations out of the firebase (which may have come earlier if the firebase was intended to be very temporary in nature).
8. Structures built above ground for long-term occupation.
9. Evacuation, including demolition of fortifications and removal of anything potentially of use to the enemy.

OPPOSITE **Building a firebase**

After the initial landing to secure the perimeter, the next task was to dig it in and fly in guns (such as the 155mm howitzer being landed by a Chinook here), ammunition, HQ equipment and every other type of stores. Much of the heavy earth-moving would be done by a bulldozer, and

bunkers would initially be excavated by explosives; but even so there was still plenty of hard digging to be done by hand, with pick, shovel and entrenching tool. The jungle also had to be cleared all around the perimeter, and then re-cleared when it started to grow back. The work of building, in fact, was never ending.

Son 719 in Laos, February 8–March 25, 1971, it was found that every single clearing or hilltop where a helicopter could land was commanded by at least an enemy machine gun, and sometimes anti-helicopter mines that were activated by the downdraft of a Huey as it landed. In this operation, unlike any earlier battle in the war, the NVA also deployed 23mm, 37mm and 57mm antiaircraft guns. Taken together, all these weapons destroyed no less than 107 Freeworld aircraft in the space of 45 days, not to mention 544 helicopters damaged – certainly strongly reinforcing the idea that "happiness is a cold LZ." American observers also sighted a grand total of some 66 tanks, which posed a particularly potent threat to any LZ before it had been properly fortified with a tank threat in mind. Firebase 31 (north of Aloui on Route 9) had already been the scene of the first tank vs. tank combat of the war on February 19, when six NVA T-54s and sixteen PT-76s were destroyed for no loss of ARVN M41s. However on February 25 the ARVN garrison of the firebase was attacked by three waves of tanks and infantry in daylight, and eventually overrun – although admittedly this was the only firebase to be lost in the operation as a whole.

From the point of view of the troops who landed first, it was the fear of the unknown – the dread that they might hit a "hot" LZ – which meant that any air assault had to be taken very seriously and properly planned. This in turn helped to ensure that for most firebases there were relatively few problems with reconnaissance and insertion, and it was the exception rather than the rule for large enemy formations to be ready to attack as quickly as they had at both X-Ray and Coral, and then again during *Lam Son 719*. In many cases the firebase could complete its whole lifespan without suffering any serious attack at all, leaving it free to fulfill its mission as a base of fire and a secure LZ for troop movements in and out.

The primary purpose of the artillery and mortars in a firebase was to fire at a distance in support of infantry patrols or other operations, such as road convoys, or to help defend the perimeters of neighboring firebases. Sometimes the guns might be used for harassment and interdiction (H&I) fire, which was plotted off the map without specific target intelligence, and hence popularly known as "killing trees." Nevertheless they also always had the secondary purpose of firing at relatively close range in defense of their own firebase, sometimes against enemy mortar or rocket-firing sites, or the routes used by enemy troops before or

Manually charting fire data at the FDC in FSB Anzio, Thua Thien province, January 1969. Note that the bunker is open to the sky, at least at this level; although there would be a bombproof bunker below in case of attack. (US National Archives)

Instaling telephone cable at the tall, fortified FDC at FSB Anzio, Thua Thien province. As well as sandbags, a high proportion of the protection comes from earth- or laterite-filled steel cylinders previously used to hold artillery propellant, with both being held in place by steel pickets originally intended for barbed-wire fencing. (US National Archives)

after an attack. In moments of extreme crisis they might even fire over open sights at very close range indeed, using canister or flechette rounds (US XM546 "Beehive," or ANZAC "Splintex"), which could all be devastating. An even more fiendish technique was developed in the 25th Division called "Killer Junior," by which time-fused 105mm or 155mm shells were prepared and individually calculated so that they would burst at about 30 feet above the ground at ranges between 200m and 1,000m from the gun positions. "Killer Senior" was the same thing using 8in. howitzers. In other cases, such as the defense of the Khe Sanh combat base in 1968, a variety of other prearranged box barrages and walking or "creeping" barrages were employed to scour the glacis of a firebase under attack.

However the artillery was to be used, one thing that became particularly characteristic of the war in Vietnam was what became known as the "6,400 mil concept," or in other words the ability to shift the direction of fire rapidly to any of the 360 points of the compass. On every firebase each gun pit was circular and optimized for swiveling the guns round; and in each battery position the six gun pits were arranged as a "star" with a gun at each of the five points and the sixth gun at the center, rather than the conventional "line" formation designed to fire in just one general direction. In conceptual terms this required a reorientation of training both for each gun crew and for the way fire-control data was handled. For example it needed bigger map boards and charts in the battery's Fire Direction Center (FDC). In physical terms it was found to be fairly difficult to "swivel" the old M101A1 towed 105mm howitzer through 6,400 mils, because it weighed about 2½ tons and its split trail had to be man-handled laboriously. With its new lightweight replacement, the M102, swiveling was very much easier because the gun weighed just 1½ tons and had a unified trail. For the M114A1 towed 155mm howitzer a special pedestal was developed by the ingenious Lt Nathaniel Foster of 8th Battalion, 6th Artillery, to facilitate rotation. With the SP 105mm, 155mm, 175mm and 8in. pieces, of course, tactical mobility was provided by their motorized (and armored) tracked chassis, although these same chassis made the weapons too heavy to be lifted by helicopters. In Vietnam the much lighter towed 105mm and 155mm guns were much handier and easier to deploy, even though they were already obsolete for the purposes of civilized armored warfare in Europe.

OPPOSITE **Multiple layers of defense**

A well-developed firebase would have numerous structures above ground level, which would all be vulnerable to incoming fire from mortars or rockets. Yet the firebase itself would have multiple layers of defense as well as awesome firepower, which could be enhanced by modern electronic surveillance technologies including radar and starlight scopes. To the left of this illustration is an AN/MPQ-4 counter-mortar radar on a timber tower; an O-1 Bird Dog FAC spotter plane flies over the 105mm howitzer pits, M113 APC and M48 tank, looking for "Charlie."

The enormous defensive strength of a firebase in Vietnam rested on a large number of different elements, which were all designed to come together to create an impenetrable lethal zone all around the perimeter. Anyone attempting to cross this zone would be hit by an overwhelming volume of what Gen Westmoreland once memorably stated was the key to the whole war in Vietnam, namely "firepower." The infantry manning the perimeter would fire their rifles, machine guns and M79 grenade launchers, and throw other grenades by hand. The artillery, mortars and recoilless rifles sited at the center of the position would also join in, as would any armored vehicles present, such as upgunned M113 armored cavalry assault vehicles (ACAV), or SP antiaircraft guns (M42A1 "Duster" dual 40mm, or truck-mounted M55 quad .50-cal. machine guns). Nor would that be the end of the story. Trip flares, Claymore mines and booby traps would be activated in the belts of barbed wire surrounding the base, and artillery fire would be called down from neighboring firebases, or sometimes from warships offshore. Then air support would arrive in all its multiple forms: helicopter gunships, fixed-wing flareships or gunships, and fixed-wing strike aircraft, both slow-moving propeller-driven and fast jets, maybe even including B-52s of the Strategic Air Command.

Merely to list all these sources of firepower is impressive enough in itself, but they all had to be used to maximum effect, and this meant good coordination between them from the very start, often even before the firebase had actually been built. As Robert J. Nicoli stated in 1969, "It is mandatory that close coordination and cooperation be established at the earliest possible time between the engineer commander, the artillery commander and the infantry commander." Not only did the direct-fire weapons have to be sited carefully, and on suitable

A large, sandbagged bunker complex used as living quarters at FSB Anzio, Thua Thien province, incorporating a steel Conex box at bottom right. (US National Archives)

The crew of an M114A1 155mm howitzer resting between fire missions, June 1969. Note the white-painted ammunition tubes used as markers at the four points of the compass, to assist orientation according to the "6,400 mil" concept. Still more helpful, from the crews' viewpoint, is the speed jack supporting the central point of the gun, thereby greatly easing the labor of swiveling it to a new direction, as well as allowing the hard standing beneath the gun to be smaller in area. (US National Archives)

soil, to give interlocking fields of fire, but the indirect-fire weapons and aircraft would require good airspace management. Shells could not be fired through the same part of the airspace at the same time it was being used by helicopters or other aircraft, so someone had to plan and coordinate everything that was going on. There was also a need to give detailed clearance to fire into any area where civilians or troops from other friendly units might be present. MACV had issued some detailed rules of engagement designed to minimize accidents, although they also greatly added to the headaches of the targeteers.[6] All this in turn demanded good command and control arrangements, so every firebase would have a command post (CP) or tactical operations center (TOC) in which these functions could be carried out by the artillery's forward observers or liaison officers. Firebases containing a battery or more would have a larger and more specialized FDC, or a fire support co-ordination center (FSCC). At battalion or brigade levels there would also be aircraft warning centers responsible for negotiating priorities as between the Army and the Air Force. Often the Army would be allowed to manage all the airspace; in some cases its remit went up only to 5,000ft, and in areas of greatest air activity the Air Force took control of all the airspace.

For fire control to be effective, a plentiful array of good radios was required, which in turn often implied numerous antennae, masts and even towers for optimum transmission. These would be particularly vulnerable to incoming fire during an attack, however well dug-in the radios and their operators might be underneath them, so they made a somewhat weak spot in the defenses. Something similar could also be said of ancillary electronic equipments such as NODs, short-range anti-personnel radars (held by infantry), AN/MPQ-4 mortar-locating radars (issued to artillery battalions), AN/TPS-25 ground surveillance radars (issued to divisional artillery), or searchlights for either white light or infrared illumination. All of these instruments could be tied directly into the FDC, so that the information they generated could be fed directly into the artillery fireplans of the base.

The purpose of all this equipment was to identify targets accurately for the defenders' artillery and mortars; but they were delicate machines and by their nature they had to be emplaced above ground level, which made them excellent targets for the enemy. Timber towers had to be built to accommodate

[6] See Ott, David Ewing *Field Artillery, 1954–73*, pp. 173–79ff.

Field artillery digital computer (FADAC) at the FDC of FSB Tomahawk (somewhere in I CTZ), April 10, 1971. The first genuine computers for fire direction had appeared during World War II, and much technical progress had been made since then – but vastly less than has been made in the years between 1971 and the present day. (US National Archives)

the AN/MPQ-4 in particular. They could also be unpopular with their own operators, who might find them more trouble than they were worth, especially the AN/MPQ-4, which had a narrow arc of scan and was entirely ineffective against low-trajectory rockets. In a 1969 study it was found to be able to locate less than 20 percent of the enemy mortars firing in its area, sometimes because the enemy was deliberately locating his firing points outside the radar's arc. In practice the radar was often more useful, in the days before GPS, to confirm the exact location of friendly mortars or even, if a helicopter was sent to hover over a particular spot, the location of troops in the field or particular features of the terrain. As with so many electronic devices used in this war, the AN/MPQ-4 represented a "first generation" of technological development, and was subject to all manner of "bugs" that would not be fully sorted out until a whole new generation had passed.

Prefabricated timber-frame structures, widely used in building bunkers and other facilities in firebases. (US National Archives)

The same was true to an even greater extent of the multiple sensors that made up the "electronic battlefield" that began to be deployed in late 1967 and early 1968 in the Demilitarized Zone (DMZ – ironically the scene of some of the most ferocious fighting anywhere in this war). The plan had been to build a "McNamara Wall" by sowing the whole area with assorted air-delivered unmanned seismic, acoustic, magnetic and other devices that could detect any movement (and its direction, length of column etc.) with sufficient accuracy to target artillery or air strikes, thereby reducing the need for garrisons and mobile sweeps on the ground. However, the Tet Offensive preempted these plans, and many of the sensors were reassigned to the defense of the Khe Sanh Combat Base. Once the siege there had been lifted, they were used instead on the Ho Chi Minh Trail in Laos and Cambodia, as well as around the perimeters of selected firebases in South Vietnam. Of these, enemy attacks were predicted and preemptively beaten off by elements of 25th Division northwest of Saigon at FSB Malone on March 15, 1969 and then, more famously, at FSB Crook on June 5–7, 1969.

The "electronic battlefield" could sometimes provide dramatic early warning of an enemy attack; but normally its performance was patchy or unsatisfactory. It was largely a technology for the future. For the present, the main way to monitor enemy movements in the area of a firebase was the time-honored use of infantry patrols and ambushes. These were doubly effective when they enjoyed good relations with a local civilian population, or with ARVN authorities, who could supply timely human intelligence; but in many areas of operations neither were available. In any case, patrolling was always very hard work for the infantry concerned, not only because of the heat, the difficulties of the terrain and the vulnerability to surprise attack, but especially because, to be effective, they had to be maintained constantly, all the year round. In some cases when the infantry was nervous, they preferred to remain inside the perimeter of their firebases and conduct reconnaissance by fire with a "mad minute" at dawn and dusk during which they fired their rifles and machine guns into the surrounding areas where the enemy might be lurking. The infantry could also be supplemented by airborne surveillance from various types of helicopter reconnaissance teams, or fixed-wing aircraft using side looking airborne radar (SLAR) or, later, infra-red equipment; but once again there was no certainty that all enemy preparations would be detected. Almost all the measures required to find them were proactive, and therefore more difficult to organize on a daily basis than the reactive defenses at which firebases excelled.

March 21, 1970: a member of 13th Signal Bn, 1st Air Cavalry, at work in FSB Buttons (Phuoc Long province), which was a base sophisticated enough and big enough to include a landing strip capable of taking fixed-wing aircraft. The bewildering "spaghetti" of wires inside this advanced communication bunker speaks volumes about the high state-of-the-art electronics that were deemed necessary to suppress what was, after all, a relatively unsophisticated enemy. (US National Archives)

Firebases had to accept that if an attack did materialize, there might well be no early warning at all; but only a "late warning" – usually late at night – in the shape of an incoming mortar and rocket barrage, accompanied by black-pajama'd enemy sappers crawling into the wire to cut it and neutralize the trip flares and Claymore mines. In these circumstances the initial reaction to the attack would depend on the traditional military qualities required from all garrisons down the ages, such as the alertness of sentries, the speed at which sleeping soldiers could wake up and man their weapons, and the solidity of the basic defensive architecture. If the defenses were not properly laid out to bring down fire rapidly all around the perimeter, or if the troops lacked adequate overhead cover and breastworks against direct fire, then an attacker might be able to win significant footholds in their midst before a suitable reaction could be organized.

If the first principle of firebase defense was "firepower," then the second was undoubtedly "digging." Even when an infantry company set up the smallest and most temporary type of firebase of all, a night defensive position (NDP), each man would scoop out at least a shallow shell scrape to protect his prone body from direct fire and flying splinters. In anything intended to be more permanent, even if only for a week or two, full trenches, bunkers and overhead cover would be mandatory, as well as thick and multilayered wire obstacles. It would not be long before a bulldozer, coils of razor wire and its picket stakes, chain-link fencing to act as anti-rocket screens, sandbags, timber, corrugated steel and pierced steel planking (PSP) would be helicoptered in, together with all manner of scrounged or recycled items for which some sort of fortification use might be found. Empty ammunition boxes, or the steel tubes and cylinders that had been used

2nd Bn, 8th Regiment, 1st Air Cavalry working on underground bunkers at a VHF site at FSB Jay (probably the one in Tay Ninh province, in preparation for the incursion into Cambodia), March 21, 1970. The "airmobile" concept is illustrated by the Chinook helicopter bringing in artillery while a Huey has already landed on an LZ. Filled ammo boxes held in place by picket stakes are being used in the fortifications, and there is good overhead cover. Berms have been bulldozed around the emplaced 105mm howitzers. The only obvious weakness in the position is the close proximity of the treeline. (US National Archives)

A well-constructed timber-framed observation tower for a searchlight, including corrugated steel roof and plentiful sandbags. Presumably an underground bunker would be at its base (1st Bn, 21st Artillery, 1st Air Cavalry, May 1967). (US National Archives)

as packing for artillery propellants, were especially widely used. As time went on and the firebase became increasingly "permanent," an ever increasing list of building materials would be brought in, ranging from cement and concrete to steel CONEX boxes which, given a little judicious welding, could be provided with a few firing slits to convert them into improvised pillboxes.[7]

By about 1969 the Americans had developed a "standard operating procedure" for siting the bunkers for an infantry company, around a firebase perimeter. This involved a 40m rope stuck into the center of the base, at the end of which the sites for a total of 24 bunkers would be staked out: one at every 15° around the circumference of the position. At each bunker site a 15 lb. shaped charge would be used to blow a hole in the ground, which would then be dug out to make a 9ft. square inhabitable space, which was then given overhead cover with two sheets of steel planking covered by sandbags. Inside this line of infantry positions a bulldozer would dig out command bunkers and berms for gun positions and maybe additional berms around an inner "keep" or final defensive redoubt. Beyond the outer infantry line, triple concertina wire would be laid out in a circle at 115m from the center of the position.

No less important than the need to dig in the inhabitants of a firebase was the need to clear an open field of fire in front of their perimeter. In some terrains it could pose a major engineering task. Robert Nicoli, serving with the Marines in 1968–69, said that in order to clear all the ground for a firebase in jungle, including its glacis, the following stores would normally be required:

- 1,000 lb. of composition C-4 explosives
- 10 cases of bangalore torpedoes
- 5,000ft of detonating cord
- 500ft of time fuse
- 300 non-electric blasting caps
- 100 M-60 fuze lighters

He added that, "Along with this allowance of demolitions, specific items of engineer equipment and hand tools are required to be used in clearing the area of trees and brush … The specific items from these tool kits which are of the most value in FSB development are the axes, brush hooks, machetes, shovels, post hole diggers, and log carriers. The gasoline engine-driven chain saw rounds out the list of those items initially lifted into the site. It is normal to plan to have from 3 to 6 chain saws."

All of the above represented the precautions and fortifications necessary to beat off an enemy attack at moments of crisis, which on some occasions could be intense. However the more "permanent" a firebase became, the more it would be able to allow itself the luxury of buildings above ground level, in which the garrison could live their everyday lives during the 99 percent of their time when they were not under attack. Mess halls, common rooms, barracks and storerooms might fall into this category, allowing the inhabitants to enjoy a more civilized lifestyle than when they had to live in nothing better than tents or holes in the ground. Such structures might be partially fortified at best, and therefore still very vulnerable to mortar or rocket fire. They would have to be regarded as "expendable" in a crisis, when the hope would be that their inhabitants would be able to reach a bunker before it was too late.

---

[7] A specific inventory of the types of materials typically used in these fortifications may be found in Gordon L. Rottman's study of *Special Forces Camps in Vietnam 1961–70*, Osprey Fortress No.33.

The operational use of firebases

We have already noted that to set down a firebase there was a need for proper reconnaissance and planning, as well as plenty of helicopters to land an initial garrison and its stores quickly, before the enemy could react. Once that initial insertion had occurred, the firebase could be made almost completely impregnable to attack within a very short time. In operational terms this was of enormous importance to the Freeworld side, because it meant they could move their troops and artillery to almost any part of the theater of war that they desired, at relatively short notice. By using floating gun platforms and pontoons, firebases could even be established in rivers and swamps where no installations were possible on the ground. The US Navy's brown water navy also provided an array of specialized armored boats to allow Task Force 117 (Mobile Riverine Force) to operate as a brigade group up and down the tricky channels and puzzling terrain of the Mekong Delta.

The problem, however, was that moving troops from one place to another was not necessarily the same thing as defeating the enemy. It was always open to him to retreat and fade away into the jungle. It would then be necessary to chase him into his own strongholds by sweeps on the ground, originally described as "search and destroy" missions but then renamed in a number of ways to make them sound more palatable to the US home public ("search and clear," "search and attack," etc.) Even then, it would still be open to the enemy to fade away yet again in front of the sweep. The Freeworld troops could only rarely force a battle upon the enemy if he did not choose to stand and fight.

If he did stand and fight, the difficulty was that although VC and NVA strongholds could never be made anything like as impregnable as the Freeworld firebases, they could still often put up enough stubborn resistance to overstretch the attacking troops. In a few cases they could even survive several operations against them; for example the NVA was never entirely forced out of the A Shau Valley, and the difficulty of clearing the tunnels of Cu Chi are legendary. VC and NVA strongholds were quite often virtually undetectable until the point platoon of a search and destroy mission blundered into them or, in other words, was ambushed by them. Whereas a Freeworld firebase would always be obvious to all as a "built-up area" in the middle of a cleared field of fire, the enemy would go to great lengths to conceal and camouflage his bunkers, trenches and tunnel systems, hiding them in deep undergrowth whenever possible.[8]

Firefights within a prepared enemy stronghold area were therefore likely to start on terms favorable to the enemy, and for that reason the attack might be stalled. Since the normal tactical unit for a Freeworld offensive sweep was usually just one infantry company, it was not uncommon for the defenders to have superior numbers and combat power at the point of contact. The Freeworld forces would usually be light infantry brought in by helicopter, without armor in support, so they would be fighting with essentially the same types of weapons as the communists. They would also be standing in the open, whereas

Mess hall, 1st Bn, 8th Artillery, 25th Infantry Division, after heavy rains during the Cambodia incursion, May 1970. The temporary nature of the structures is very evident, as is the chaotic problem of accommodating large volumes of logistic stores during a mobile operation. (US National Archives)

---

[8] See Gordon L. Rottman's treatment of these systems in Osprey Fortress No. 48: *Viet Cong and NVA Tunnels and Fortifications of the Vietnam War.*

An aerial view of FSB Thu Thua (Long An province), May 1969, showing the "6,400 mil" layout of its six-gun battery, and the cleared glacis. This appears to be a well-settled and "permanent" camp. (US National Archives)

the enemy would be carefully dug-in below ground level. Air strikes, or artillery fire from the nearest firebase, would doubtless be called down to help in the battle. However, efficient enemy overhead cover could go far towards neutralizing its effects. If the firefight was taking place at very short range in thick bush, moreover, the really heavy firepower would often be unable to reach the enemy troops fighting in the very front line, due to the safety distances that had to be observed in front of friendly troops. For this reason, whether in attack or defense, it was always the aim of the VC and NVA to use "hugging" tactics in their firefights, to get as close as possible to their opponents and inside the zone of immunity from heavy long-range weaponry.

In these circumstances the Freeworld infantry would often be fighting at a disadvantage on ground of the enemy's choosing. Even if they did finally succeed in clearing the position and inflicting heavy casualties, they would still find that the VC and NVA troops were expert in the art of exfiltration from the battlefield, either as individuals or in small groups. They would also often find ways to remove as many as possible of their own killed and wounded to pre-arranged rendezvous sites quite a few kilometers away from the battlefield. There the survivors would regroup, rearm, bury the dead and treat the wounded. Only rarely would the Freeworld side have the strength and determination to follow up so far from the area they had originally been searching. Thus the communist forces were usually able to make their units as hard to seize as possible, thereby keeping the initiative in their own hands. This was the whole essence of guerrilla tactics.

The role of firebases in search and destroy operations was to provide LZs, command and control facilities and jumping-off points for the searching troops, as well as staging points for supplies and, especially, firing points for supporting mortars and artillery. Firebases were therefore essential back-ups to any offensive operations, even though those operations themselves might be

A tin rain shelter over a relatively large sandbagged FDC at FSB Concord (Bien Hoa province), May 1969 (Battery A, 7th Bn, 9th Artillery). Note the alarm on the pole and raised timber platform for surveillance equipment to the right. (US National Archives)

putting their participants in harm's way in the face of an evasive foe. Yet when they were thrown onto the defensive by a determined enemy attack, firebases might sometimes take on an even more important tactical role in their own right. Because they were all but invulnerable, they represented an excellent way to inflict terrific and terrible casualties upon anyone who chose to attack them, and often far more in a single night than a major offensive sweep might hope to achieve in a week. Firebases were often a source of the most extreme violence that could be found anywhere in this whole violent war.

The extraordinary thing, perhaps, is that the communists attempted to attack as many firebases as they actually did, since whenever they did so, it was they who would be "fighting at a disadvantage on ground of the enemy's choosing." The record

shows that they could not attack a Freeworld firebase without inevitably suffering enormous casualties, and almost always their attack would be repulsed. So why did they keep on making the effort? There are three main reasons. Firstly the VC/NVA normally enjoyed excellent intelligence of the layout of firebases, which were never deliberately camouflaged (although the rapid regrowth of vegetation might sometimes conceal minor details of wire barriers and mines in the firebase perimeter). In some cases the VC might even have agents working within the firebase as washerwomen or laborers. Thus they might be encouraged by their great knowledge of the enemy dispositions and weak spots. At LZ Bird, for example, (see pp.36–37) they knew full well that the defenses were very weak, and so their decision to attack must be seen as militarily correct.

Secondly, it was always the intention of the North Vietnamese high command to keep up as much pressure as possible on the Americans and their running dogs. If the Americans did not oblige by entangling themselves in offensive sweeps against VC/NVA strongholds, then the war would have to be carried back to them by launching sacrificial attacks on their firebases. Even if this meant accepting massive losses, it might well inflict some casualties upon the other side. These would impress upon the home public in the USA not only that the demand for Vietnamese reunification was insistent, but that resisting it would always incur a certain cost in terms of GIs being flown home in body bags. It has to be said that in political terms, as early as mid 1968 this shockingly "sacrificial" version of attritional strategy had indeed become entirely successful.

Thirdly and finally, there was never any intention to make a bloody assault on a Freeworld firebase unless the communist side believed it could afford to lose all (i.e. 100 percent) of the troops it committed to the assault. In operational terms, the key point to make is that it was always the VC/NVA who chose to attack a firebase, rather than the firebase somehow being able to force them to attack. Thus, once again, the operational initiative lay with the communists. To put it another way, they could always control their own rate of attrition. When Gen Westmoreland stated that he wanted to win the war by inflicting unacceptable attrition on the enemy, he had not stopped to reflect that he had no really effective method of forcing the enemy to accept heavy casualties unless the enemy himself felt that he could afford to lose them.

Assuming a firebase had been completed, it was far more likely to be attacked during the hours of darkness than in daylight, according to the old tag that "the night belongs to Charlie." Under the threat of massive aerial surveillance and attack, the communists were forced to assemble their assault forces in the most clandestine manner possible, taking advantage of whatever cover was available from darkness, vegetation or some other artifice. Often they would be able to

A complex array of antennae and other communications equipment at an elevated hilltop position, 4th Infantry Divison, June 5, 1969. Once again we find that the vital electronic part of a firebase's function was necessarily the least well protected from enemy fire. By the same token the sparse scattering of sandbags over the corrugated steel roofing was designed to hold it down in high winds rather than to afford protection against mortar bombs. (US National Archives)

Air-delivered seismic intrusion detectors (ADSIDs) on show in the Ho Chi Minh Trail Museum in the outskirts of Hanoi, 2004. This family of sensors was used in the defense of the Khe Sanh combat base in Quang Tri province, and then, among others, FSB Malone and FSB Crook in Tay Ninh province. (Ed Flint and Paul Harris)

infiltrate their leading infantry and sappers at least as far forward as the firebase wire, and even some way through it, before the alarm was sounded. A major part of the tactical problem facing the defenders was therefore to find ways of turning night into day. As in earlier 20th-century wars, this was done mainly with pyrotechnics such as Verey lights or parachute flares (either projected up into the sky by rockets, mortars or artillery, or dropped down from it by aircraft); and sometimes by the careful use of searchlights.

Perhaps the most effective way to "turn night into day" consisted of the fixed-wing flareship, which was known by all sorts of exotic names ranging from "Smokey the Bear" to "Puff the Magic Dragon," depending on its specific type. It was designed to combine the well-established concept of dropping parachute flares from the air with the very novel idea of flying in tight circles around the illuminated area, while firing electrically operated Vulcan guns with an exceptionally high rate of fire (and sometimes even 105mm howitzers). Not only could such an aircraft illuminate the battlefield at night, but it could also "turn the jungle into a tossed green salad." It was originally deployed mainly to beat down nighttime movements on the Ho Chi Minh Trail; but its value was also proved in a number of firebase defense battles, not least at FSPB Coral in May 1968 and FSB Crook on June 5–7, 1969. There was, however, a problem: a flareship would not usually be activated unless a specific alarm had already been sounded. In other words, it was not used to detect the original approach of the enemy, but only to illuminate and shoot him up once his presence had become known. To detect his presence in the first place, it was necessary to rely on sentries equipped with a variety of different types of surveillance equipment, ranging from the "Mark One Eyeball" to starlight scopes and then all the way through to radars or seismic, acoustic or magnetic sensors.

LZ Bird in the Christmastide battle

As an example of what might happen when the enemy attacked a firebase, let us consider the case of LZ Bird in "the Christmastide battle" on December 26–27, 1966.[9] LZ Bird had earlier been opened in the 1st Cavalry Division's area of operations, north of An Khe, during Operation *Masher/White Wing* at the start of the year. It had a weak garrison of only half an infantry company (confusingly, a part of 12th "Cavalry" – i.e. "C" Company, 2nd Battalion), protecting two batteries of artillery (one 105mm and one 155mm). The NVA 22nd Regiment had been hoping to attack it during the moonless night of December 23; but their march into the battle area was delayed by heavy rain and problems of communication. Nevertheless, they were deployed and ready by 1830 hrs on the 26th, with their lead battalion (the 8th) as close as 12m from the US perimeter. By 2200 hrs they had laid telephone cables to link their three battalions and supporting troops, and by 2300 hrs their mortars and recoilless rifles were all in position and still undetected.

LZ Bird was 250m long with a 600m circumference; but because it was almost surrounded on three sides by a river in flood and sandbars, the garrison (a total of just 154 drowsy men, after their Christmas festivities) simply did not believe it could be attacked. Therefore no advanced sentries or listening posts had been set out, even though there were in fact viable lines of approach from high ground to the north and northeast, where the elephant grass and bamboo came

9 See Marshall, S.L.A. *Bird, the Christmastide Battle* (New York, 1968).

close to the perimeter. The perimeter itself was marked by a trench with some trip flares and Claymores; but there was no wire and no specific fire positions. In any case the garrison was too weak to have manned many. The perimeter was thus to all intents and purposes open to the NVA to walk over as it wished. Another weakness of the defenses was that there was no other clearing for miles around that might be used for an LZ by airborne reinforcements. At least the two artillery batteries each had their own fortified "redoubt" inside the perimeter, defended by fighting bunkers and infantry positions.

The attack started at 0105 hrs on the 17th, with mortar bombs landing in the center of the position, immediately followed by an infantry rush – although in fact the NVA infantry appeared to be poorly trained, poorly co-ordinated, and suffered casualties to their own mortars. But the LZ's guns, FDCs and living quarters were soon overrun in confused fighting as the (fiercely resisting) garrison was slowly forced back to the southwest corner of the position. There was also command confusion, since the US infantry and artillery commanders failed to agree on tactics. At least a radio signal was sent to the outside world within the first two minutes, although the radio was then promptly knocked out of action. The supporting artillery from LZ Pony soon joined the battle with

OVERLEAF **Mounting an operation from a firebase**

The central purpose of a firebase was not only to deliver artillery and mortar fire, and to attract enemy attacks that could be mown down by superior firepower; but also to act as a base from which offensive sweeps could be mounted into the surrounding terrain. Such operations, including the one illustrated here, might aim to create a new firebase that would, naturally, be in range of and covered by the artillery of the original base. Major problems could arise if the airspace was not properly managed, i.e. if artillery shells were being fired into the

same part of the sky through which the assault helicopters – both gunships (Huey Cobras, marked "15" here) and troop transports (Huey Slicks, three to the right here) – were attempting to fly. It was the responsibility of the fire direction center (FDC) of the firebase to orchestrate all the different agencies in order to avoid accidents. Also seen here (to the right of the Cobra) is a light observation helicopter. The inset at bottom left shows one of the base's semi-fortified huts, with its corrugated steel roof, wooden section walls, and partially sandbagged exterior base.

Mounting an operation from a firebase

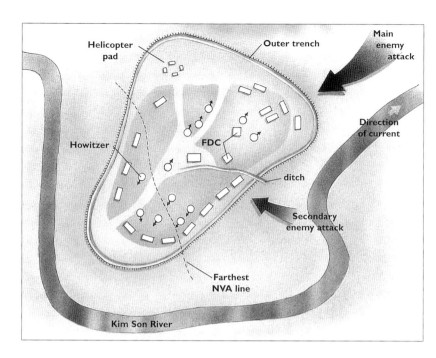

LZ Bird, Binh Dinh province, in "the Christmastide battle" on December 26, 1966. (Peter Dennis)

high-explosive (HE) and illumination rounds as the NVA kept on advancing, shouting "Yankee you die tonight! Yankee go home! What you do now, GI?"

What the Yankees did do next was to fire Beehive rounds into the faces of their attackers, from one of the few remaining 105mm howitzers. This was a very new munition at the time, and its likely effects were not well known; but they turned out to be spectacular. With each round 8,500 flechettes flew out

Diagram of FSB Crook on June 5–7, 1969. (Peter Dennis)

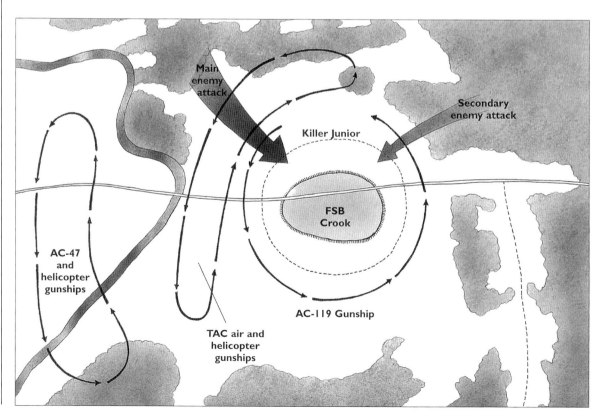

"Freq Freak" – a Mark 69 communications van at FSB Sedgwick (a.k.a Mole City, Tay Ninh province), August 15, 1969. Note the defense given to the tires by dirt-filled ammo boxes. In the background is a characteristic timber tower for surveillance apparatus – in this case apparently a searchlight. Neither the van nor the tower have anything like adequate protection against mortars, rockets or even small arms. (US National Archives)

of the muzzle of the cannon in a 30° cone of red-hot steel splinters, piercing anything and anyone to a range of 300m. The enemy was literally stopped dead in his tracks. The survivors began to pull back, while the firebase defenders were able to reopen their communications and call in ARA as well as more accurate field artillery from LZ Pony, especially to harass the enemy's line of retreat. Continuous rain made air operations difficult; but some 424 rockets were fired from helicopters, including from two sorties by the fearsome "Go Go Bird" – an experimental Chinook "air battleship" or "super gunship."[10]

When reinforcements were finally flown in from 9th Cavalry, a total of 310 enemy dead were found in and around LZ Bird, whereas the US garrison had lost as many as 135 casualties (wounded as well as killed), or more than three quarters of the original garrison. Nevertheless Bird was not fully overrun, and the enemy attack was definitely defeated. Of wider significance was the triumphant demonstration of the Beehive flechette round, which immediately became the ultimate weapon by which artillery gun pits could defend themselves over open sights at close range.

---

[10] Alas the "Go Go" experiment was later judged to be a failure for reasons outside the "Bird" battle, and two out of the three Chinooks involved in it were eventually lost.

A poorly protected water purification plant connected to bowser trailers at the sprawling and muddy FSB Bastogne, Thua Thien province, with a fully dug-in command bunker just behind it. Water is a basic necessity for life, and securing a supply of it has been an essential feature of all fortifications since the very beginning of time. (US National Archives)

FSB Crook, June 5–7, 1969

If LZ Bird was almost a defeat for the defenders, the case of FSB Crook, on June 5–7, 1969, stands as a classic example of the almost effortless ease with which a firebase could sometimes destroy its attackers. It was manned by just one infantry company and one battery, but in three days of fighting it achieved a bodycount estimated at 400 communists dead, as against just one US soldier, who was killed by mortar fire. FSB Crook was located southeast of Tay Ninh, some 80km north of Saigon (and it was, incidentally, the only firebase to have that name). It was intended to assist US operations up to the Cambodian border, to block enemy movements in the area, and even to attract attacks – as a sort of "bait" – so that maximum attrition could be inflicted. By early June a major attack was suspected, so the firebase was put on full alert. It had an extensive range of ground sensors, laid in concentric circles at 150m and 300m around the perimeter, and others further afield. Also there were night vision devices, naval binoculars and a radar tower, not to mention air and artillery assets on call from other firebases in the province.

Sure enough enemy movement was detected late on June 5, especially from the northeast and northwest, at ranges as far out as almost a kilometer. The defensive firepower immediately opened up, including "Killer Junior," helicopter gunships, a circling fixed-wing gunship, and fast jets. The full gamut of artillery was called in, including 8in. and 175mm. Taken together, all this weight of firepower managed to beat off the attackers before more than a few of them were able to penetrate the perimeter wire – and none of them got any further forward than that. Then on the following night they attacked again in greater strength; but again met the same fate. On the third night there was a renewed but much weaker attack, after which the enemy retreated to lick his wounds. During the following two decades this entirely one-sided action would frequently be cited by advocates of "the electronic battlefield" as a showpiece demonstration of just how powerful their new technology could be, in rather the same way that the British tank corps celebrated their battle of Cambrai in 1917, or all the world's nuclear strategists were forced to use the bombing of Hiroshima in 1945 as their primary reference point.

Tour of a firebase: design and developments

The essence of a firebase was its artillery, which would normally consist of one or more batteries of six guns, normally all of the same caliber; although sometimes a battery might include a mixture of two types (e.g. 105mm and 155mm, or perhaps interchangeable 175mm and 8in. barrels using the same SP chassis). Each gun would be emplaced in a circular gun pit, surrounded by a bulldozed berm, a sandbagged bank or some other type of cover, in which the inner wall would incorporate a variety of different types of ammunition lockers, as well as an underground bunker into which the crew could retreat if incoming fire became too intense. There would be 55-gal barrels of water for fire-fighting, and possibly also a specially prepared sector of the gun pit wall designated for direct fire over open sights if the situation should demand it.

Connected to the gun positions by field telephone, each battery would have an FDC, which would normally be considered the firebase's "nerve center" (or centers, if there was more than one battery); certainly of equal value to the CP or TOC of the infantry garrison. The same could also be said of the communications bunker, if there was a separate one, which would be the essential center of radio signalling to the outside world. All three of the FDC, the CP/TOC and the Commo bunker would be dug in particularly deeply and securely as early as possible, since if they were to be knocked out by a mortar bomb or rocket, a very significant part of the firebase's ability to fight as a coherent whole would be destroyed. At LZ Bird they were in fact overrun by the initial enemy attack, so that the final defense was left to the heroic initiative shown by a handful of individuals, rather than to any co-ordinated plan.

Each battery position – including gun pits and FDC – would normally be arranged in a roughly circular formation, in order to facilitate the "6,400 mil concept," although peculiarities of the terrain at any given site would impose variations in particular cases. Often there would be additional berms and even wire obstacles around the battery position, to make it a sort of "inner keep" within the wider firebase perimeter. Such redoubts might well include exposed towers for observation (by binoculars, radars, searchlights etc.) or for tall radio transmission masts. There would be generators, central ammunitions stores and

The site of Khe Sanh airfield as it is today. It is bordered by a coffee plantation, which at this western end is actually higher than the landing strip, even though at the far end it falls away onto lower ground. As so often with firebases in former South Vietnam, little more than the airstrips offer obvious points of reference to the modern tourist. (Ed Flint and Paul Harris)

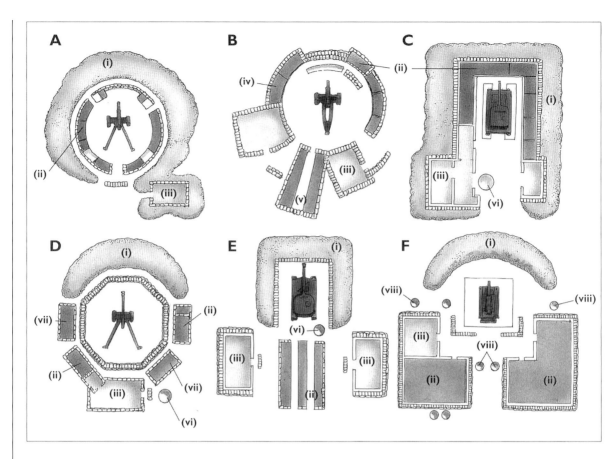

A selection of ground plans of gun pits. (Peter Dennis)

A – M101 105mm emplacement.
B – M102 105mm emplacement.
C – Semipermanent 105mm SP howitzer emplacement.
D – Towed 155mm howitzer emplacement.
E – 155mm SP howitzer emplacement.
F – Heavy artillery emplacement (8in. or 175mm).

(i) – Soft dirt.
(ii) – Ammunition racks/storage.
(iii) – Crew quarters.
(iv) – Ammunition "ready rack."
(v) – HE shell bunker.
(vi) – Powder pit.
(vii) – Powder bunker.
(viii) – Fire barrel.

fuel stores. However, the firebase's helicopter landing pad(s) would usually be outside the "keep" and even, in some cases, outside the perimeter altogether. This was determined by the need to provide a certain clear area for near-horizontal flight, especially during take-offs, as Robert J. Nicoli explained:

In order to permit the most effective use of helicopters for resupply, the EO must insure that the ground approach to, and exits from the LZ are at least as wide as two rotor diameters. These approaches must remain clear of communications wire and all other obstacles. There should also be an area clear of high obstructions (30ft or higher) extending at least 150ft in the direction of the approach and exit paths. This distance gives helicopters an opportunity to gain forward velocity before they must commence climbing.

Depending on the permanence of the base, the functional command and control centers might be supplemented by kitchens, mess halls, common rooms, bars and various other recreational facilities. These would not normally be dug in, but would be in non-tactical tents or temporary structures above ground level. The overall effect might quickly become that of a collection of untidy hutches and hootches, since regularity and neatness was usually the very last priority of soldiers anywhere near the front line, especially when many of their building materials had been scrounged from many different sources, both official and unofficial.

A special case would arise with medical aid posts, which, in those firebases that had one at all, would tend to be very small – but well dug in with overhead cover. There were some notorious exceptions: for example, the journalist Peter Braestrup confronted a general over the inadequacy of protection at the USMC Khe Sanh combat base:

General, what about the defences at Khe Sanh? Now, you built this wonderful, air conditioned officers' club and that's a complete shambles. You built a beer hall there, and that's been blown away. ... You've got a medical detachment there that's a disgrace, set up right on the airstrip, exposed to hundreds of rounds every day, and no overhead cover. (Herr, Michael *Dispatches*, p. 123)

Aid posts in the frontline would not need to be extensive. The hope would be that most of the patients could be treated quickly by a corpsman or paramedic, and immediately returned to their post of duty. If there were any serious cases, the expectation would be that they could be evacuated very quickly by a "Dustoff" helicopter to a much larger hospital far to the rear and then, if their condition remained serious, maybe flown out to an even more comprehensive base hospital, which might be as far away as Japan. It was the boast of the US medical services that, because of casualty evacuation by helicopter, only about 2 percent of the soldiers who were hit in combat would subsequently die of their wounds, provided they had not been killed outright. This in itself represented something of a revolution in "the art of war," which can stand alongside a number of other novelties of the Vietnam War, such as the concepts of helicopter assault or of "the electronic battlefield."

All the above installations represented the "central core" of a firebase but, apart from the very potent punch of artillery firing Beehive or canister rounds, and the much less certain use of rifles and pistols by officers, mess staff and signalers, there was little amongst them that could be said to contribute directly to the close defense of the firebase perimeter. That duty fell mainly to the infantry garrison, possibly reinforced by armored fighting vehicles or anti-aircraft guns firing in the ground role. Of particular importance in this would be the

An NVA sapper's view from outside the hastily laid wire at the temporary FSB Conquer (or Conquest) in Cambodia, 65km west of Pleiku, during the incursion of May 1970. Although the wire is not thick, there has nevertheless been time to build protective berms for some of the vehicles behind it. (US National Archives)

An aerial view of USMC Combat Base Elliott, astride the main road between Quang Tri and Khe Sanh, Quang Tri province, July 20, 1969. The complexity of the firebase is apparent, with a wide variety of permanent and temporary structures alongside bunkers and gun positions, as well as an unusually large number of trucks and other motor vehicles. The circular pits for the 175mm SP guns (pictured on page 20) are visible in the top right quarter of the picture, while the trench defining the defended perimeter is clearly visible on either side of the bridge to the left. (US National Archives)

OPPOSITE **M101A1 105mm gun pit in an FSB**

OPPOSITE **M101A1 105mm gun pit in an FSB**
The "business end" of a firebase was the artillery that provided the fire. Illustrated here is the inside of one of the thousands of gun pits that were built to give protection to the guns and gunners, while still allowing fire (in this case HE, as indicated by the shell colors) to be delivered to any point of the compass. In "conventional" warfare all the guns in a battery would be orientated in generally the same direction; but in the guerrilla warfare conditions of Vietnam they had to be ready to react quickly in any direction. The striped poles, as seen in the left background, indicate compass-point directions for the gunners (in this case "west").

mortars, which represented a miniature version of the artillery, using similar circular firing positions and the same "6,400 mil concept," albeit at shorter ranges. Antitank weapons might also be deployed in those cases (normally in I CTZ, from 1968 onwards) where the intervention of NVA armor might be feared.

Further out from all the central installations and heavy-weapon pits came the perimeter defenses, which would consist of a line of infantry bunkers giving interlocking fields of fire, preferably connected by a communication trench. Inside each fighting bunker there would be two or more men with M-16 rifles, M-60 machine guns and/or M-79 grenade launchers. If there was a tank threat, they might also be issued with the M-72 single shot, disposable light antitank weapon (LAW), although its backblast meant it could not be used in an enclosed space such as a bunker. Indeed, some cynics suggested that it was not usable at all, because its firing mechanism tended to be unduly affected by the damp climate.

A sawed-off mountaintop at FSB Lucas in the early stages of its construction, July 9, 1971. The battery of guns has not yet been dug into circular berms, and the field of fire, or glacis, toward the top of the picture is still curtained off by uncleared jungle. (US National Archives)

M101A1 105mm gun pit in an FSB

In front of the bunkers there was supposed to be a wide, cleared field of fire or glacis, although, for a variety of different reasons, this often proved to be inadequate if not totally nonexistent. Perhaps it was not intended to occupy a particular site for long enough to do much more than dig the troops into shallow shell scrapes, or perhaps the necessary engineering resources could not be inserted in time, for logistic reasons. Perhaps the firebase was situated on a commanding hilltop with slopes too steep to be bulldozed; or perhaps a field of fire had been cleared when the firebase was originally built, but the garrison had later allowed the vegetation to grow back to a height sufficient to conceal a battalion of crawling enemy infiltrators. The shrubs, elephant grass and variegated weeds in the hothouse climate of South Vietnam were notorious for their speed of growth at certain times of year.

Within the glacis there should be multiple lines of razor wire, preferably in great depth. The wire would be protected in turn not only by fire from the infantry bunkers, but also by a network of Claymore mines, booby traps and trip flares. Immediately before any full-scale assault, enemy sappers would attempt to neutralize as many of these as possible by a process of stealthy infiltration, and sometimes they could achieve spookily efficient results. However, they always ran a risk of detection, which would be counter-productive if it gave premature warning to the garrison that an attack was imminent, especially if it also gave away the intended direction of the attack. The risk of detection was greatly increased, from 1968 onward, in cases where unmanned sensors were laid out in front of the wire, as at FSB Crook in June 1969.

Aerial view of the USMC FSB Los Banos (Thua Thien province, on the coast near Da Nang) in April 1970. This firebase had first been occupied by 101st Airborne Division, then evacuated; then reoccupied by the Marines. It is almost a "model" for a company position built on a hilltop, enclosing a battery of M102 105mm howitzers and some mortars, including three lines of wire and anti-rocket wire mesh screens in front of major command bunkers. However, the gaps in the wire for the central road might be a defensive weakness unless they were regularly closed when the road was not in use. (US National Archives)

Hilltop retransmission site at FSB T-bone (Thua Thien province) in 1971. It commanded an excellent direct view of Hue, and hence excellent conditions for radio transmissions. Note the inner "keep" for all the clever technical stuff is at the summit (with an MPQ-4 counter-mortar radar just to the left), while the perimeter defense bunkers are scattered around the slopes below. (US National Archives)

Apart from sensors, certain additional defensive preparations might be made at ranges some way beyond the outer edges of the wire and the cleared field of fire. All likely firing points for enemy mortars and rockets, all likely approach routes for enemy infantry, and all likely sites for enemy logistic dumps, field hospitals etc. should have been reconnoitered at the same time as the firebase was built. There was a great deal that the command team in a firebase could do to predict such things and outguess the likely behavior of an attacker. Such a process would allow the artillery and mortars of the firebase to be preregistered on defensive fire programs and also, still more importantly, it would allow the air assets (Army helicopters and Air Force fixed-wing aircraft) to preplan their likely target areas in the event of an enemy assault.

The ground plan of the firebase (or "trace" in the terminology of classic fortification) might vary widely, especially according to the local contours. Some examples were almost linear, if they were laid out along the crestline of a steep razorback ridge, which might be only a few dozen meters wide. On flatter terrain they would more normally be circular, pentagonal or star shaped, particularly providing good flanking fields of fire to machine guns firing on fixed lines from salient points. FSB Patton II (Hau Nghia province) was described as "a beautiful symmetrical circle" with 24 fighting bunkers, whereas FSB Gela (Binh Duong province) was described as "like a deputy's five pointed star lying on ground with a wreath of 3 strands of concertina wire around it."[11] In many cases the layout was uncannily reminiscent of the famous European star forts or bastioned fortresses of the 17th and 18th centuries, which had been designed to deliver flanking fire from cannons for exactly the same reasons. Also following their example, the Vietnam firebases often included a central internal "citadel" or "keep" as a fallback position in case the outer perimeter should be penetrated by the enemy. Typically this would house the command, control and communications centers and therefore, perhaps, also the most highly motivated officers who might be expected to resist most strongly and hold out for longest.

A view of the other side of FSB T-bone, with its mountaintop accommodating an FM antenna field. By the time this photo was taken, the defenses had been developed to a greater degree than had been the case in the photo on the opposite page. (US National Archives)

[11] Kelly, Michael P. *Where We Were in Vietnam. A comprehensive guide to the firebases, military installations and naval vessels of the Vietnam war 1945–75*, p.5-195; from Mills, Hugh L. Jr and Anderson, Robert A. *Low Level Hell.*

Life in a firebase

Vietnam was often very hot and humid, which, in the absence of air-conditioned fieldworks, could make life very uncomfortable for the garrisons of firebases. In all the photographs in the present volume less than five of the troops can be seen wearing flak jackets, and only a minority of the rest are wearing any other type of jacket. The most favored code of dress is a bare torso, or perhaps a very light T-shirt or vest. Nor are helmets widely worn. We can infer from this that firebases were relatively safe places, and the troops manning them, at least in daylight, did not feel themselves to be under imminent threat of attack for most of the time. This would be diametrically opposite to their thoughts and fears whenever they should venture forth on a patrol or sweep outside the defended perimeter.

Of course there would be moments when a firebase garrison had to dress for war and lie low in its bunkers; sometimes for days on end if the base was under close siege and continuous fire. In these circumstances it could be a relatively unsafe place, especially if there was a shortage of communication trenches and overhead cover. Latrines were primitive and not even "piss tubes" were built everywhere. Even when the enemy stopped firing, life in a firebase would usually continue to be fairly uncomfortable. Rain might turn your personal hole into a mud bath, or the whole firebase into a shallow lake. It could weaken or wash away semipermanent constructions at the same time as it helped the vegetation to grow at an uncontrollable rate – both of which required extra fatigue parties to put right. Then again, very few of the bases smaller than Khe Sanh would have

Burning human excrement in diesel oil, in the base of a cut-down 55-gal drum, FSB Veghel, Thua Thien province, 1970. This was the standard method of hygienic disposal used in most firebase latrines. (Don Aird)

OPPOSITE **Daily life**
The troops who manned firebases were not always digging or sleeping. Many of the photographs that have come down to us show that they were often able to snatch a relaxed moment without fear of enemy attack, so the wearing of helmets and flak jackets would be considered unnecessary. In any case, there would usually be protected places into which the troops could dive quickly if they came under fire. Shown here is a mail call, which was always a high point since it represented the troops' main link with home and the family; and chow line at a field kitchen, which provided a different type of sustenance.

Daily life

Berms at the site of 173d Airborne Brigade's base at Dak To, as they looked in 2005. They were designed to protect firebase installations and may even have accommodated helicopters. This base area has been extensively dug up by local people looking for war materials to sell as scrap, and a picture similar to this is about as much of the original excavations as one can expect to find anywhere in Vietnam. (Ed Flint and Paul Harris)

anything like shower blocks, beer halls or officers' clubs, and the food would not normally be freshly cooked at a central kitchen. Even at the gigantic "Golf Course" base in 1965 Col Moore reported, "We lived rough: pup tents, C-rations, and showers only when it rained," although he did at least insist that his men shaved daily.[12]

Apart from the heat and problems with water and food, there was always the local fauna to contend with. Lice, leeches, flies, mosquitoes and snakes could all pose threats ranging from mild inconvenience through tropical diseases to instant death. Several casualties, including at least one fatality, were also caused by tigers around FSB Alpine, in Quang Tri province. Nor was all the dangerous fauna necessarily "local." On one occasion a field kitchen was bombed by a helicopter delivering Thanksgiving turkeys that had not yet been defrosted.

One feature that comes over strongly from the photographs of firebases is that they were not usually pretty places to live in. Typically they would be covered in churned-up mud (or dustclouds when it was hot and dry), since so many people and their vehicles would have to live confined within a relatively small space. Diametrically different from the enemy's practice, no attempt would be made to camouflage the position or hide the debris. Soldiers in all wars tend to leave plenty of litter, doubtless because they have much more pressing concerns than civic tidiness when they are in action; but in Vietnam this habit tended to reach new peaks. Nor would anything approaching "aesthetic" considerations go into firebase architecture. On the contrary, there would be a general impression of a shanty town built with whatever materials happened to be at hand, both new and recycled, and more often with temporary rather than permanent buildings. Tents and mud holes would co-exist with relatively grander structures, although in this context the word "grand" might imply little more than a few layers of neatly laid sandbags. New building work of one type or another would also be almost constantly under way, and so the whole shape of the installation might change on an almost daily basis, thereby adding further to the mess and disruption.

It is a notorious fact that the experience of living in a "shanty town," or merely camping rough, can often be extremely uncomfortable, especially for

[12] Moore, Harold G. and Galloway, Joseph L. *We Were Soldiers Once ... and Young*, pp. 30, 36.

people who are not used to it. In fact shanty town environments have helped to fuel some of the most violent political uprisings in world history, and in Vietnam they doubtless played a certain role in exacerbating the widespread unrest among US troops from about 1970 onwards. Firebases were not easy places to live in, especially since almost everyone in Vietnam, on whichever side of the war, was constantly aware that an arbitrary death could strike at any time. Both sides always tried hard to maximize the element of surprise in their attacks, ambushes and explosions, quite apart from the very many unintended fatal accidents and cases of "collateral damage" that could strike at any time. In statistical terms the threats could often be more perceived than real; but the fact remains that unspecified dangers were always thought to be lurking somewhere in the middle ground of the picture, rather than merely in the background.

We must add that the geographical and cultural environment of Indochina – and actually the disciplines of military life itself – were often deeply alien to draftees airlifted straight into the jungle from the relative comforts and freedoms of cities in the USA. As a striking example of this alienation, contrary to the quite common practice in most earlier US wars around the world, in Vietnam very few Americans seemed to believe that their battle dead should be buried in military cemeteries close to where they fell. Vietnam was thought to be such a "barbaric" and "alien" country that the bodies of the fallen would be flown back to individual family funerals in their hometowns in the USA.

A typical hole, "about the size of an armchair," dug by local people desperate to find used or discarded shells and bombs on the battlefield, in order to sell the scrap metal. This one was photographed at the site of FSB Gio Linh, Quang Tri province, in 2005. (Ed Flint and Paul Harris)

A firebase under attack

OPPOSITE **A firebase under attack**
Firebases were usually attacked at night, starting with sappers crawling into the perimeter wire to cut it and deactivate the Claymore mines and trip flares. With luck the sappers would remain undetected until a savage bombardment of mortars and rockets was unleashed on the center of the base, which would be the signal for mass assaults with a battalion, or up to a whole regiment, of infantry. They would be helped forward with satchel charges, RPGs and grenades to destroy fortifications. Meanwhile the top priority for Freeworld defenders would be to "turn night into day" with parachute flares and many other types of device. Here the NVA attack can be seen encountering Claymore mines, the devastating Beehive flechette rounds, and a cone of fire from a fixed-wing gunship.

On the other side of the equation the First World troops enjoyed many amenities that are denied to most shanty dwellers; not least regular rations and excellent medical back-up. The present author has even met a French colonel who served in Vietnam up to 1954, who swore it was the most beautiful place in the entire world. Quite a holiday camp, in fact! At least until about 1970 the US forces seemed to be capable of enduring this environment perfectly well, doubtless in part due to their professionalism and solid military culture; but also in part because of their belief that they would eventually prevail. It was the growing suspicion after 1968 that the war was being lost that surely did more than anything else to undermine the faith of the troops in the field.

"Faith" could be sustained by a variety of different support structures. If they managed to make it as far forward as a firebase, padres could offer individual counseling and encouragement on a day-to-day basis, as well as running formal

A military chaplain leading prayer at an unusually non-muddy firebase in June 1968. There is something particularly incongruous and poignant about religious services that are held in the field rather than in a church, chapel or synagogue. Such occasions tend to be relatively rare in the front line, and therefore all the more powerful for participants. (US National Archives)

Dismantling the overhead cover of a bunker at the hilltop site of FSB Challenge (Binh Dinh province), June 1970. Dismantling fortifications before they were evacuated was in many ways just as important – and laborious – as building them. The (entirely justified) fear was that if the enemy got hold of almost any piece of scrap metal or disused munitions, he would convert them into new weaponry of his own. Equally if he was able to occupy ready-made bunkers on a commanding site, he could be devilishly difficult to dislodge. (US National Archives)

(and often very powerful) religious services in the field. Even if the chaplain failed to appear in person, there were regular religious broadcasts on the armed forces' radio, which also carried a variety of other patriotic and supposedly morale-building messages. More to the point, perhaps, the radio brought music into the frontline trenches in a way that had never been possible in any previous war. It was only in the 1960s that rock and roll records and portable transistor radios would come together to make a very potent mixture, even before one asked exactly what the listeners might be smoking at the time. The ready availability of cigarettes was of course itself already a time-honored morale-building factor on any battlefield, and recognized as such by the military authorities. Men in daily fear of a violent death will not be as worried as they should be by the long-term risks of cancer; but they will draw satisfaction, reassurance and calm from the nicotine, which also suppresses hunger.

After the chaplain, the radio and the cigarettes, mail from home was another potent link between the individual soldier and his wider community and culture back home. However, it could famously go wrong if there were family bereavements or girlfriend trouble that the soldier could not get away to attend to in person. Michael Herr reported a particularly bizarre case when a Marine mailed a severed ear home to his girlfriend as a souvenir, and then wondered why she stopped writing to him. As in many other wars, also, there could be problems when soldiers received newspapers from home, since the way the war was usually described in the press would almost inevitably be unrecognizable to the way it was perceived by troops in the frontline. Then again, direct reporting of the antiwar movement could be disturbing, and in extreme cases could fan the flames of combat refusal. Nevertheless, for the most part regular mail from home exerted a very positive influence on morale, and the military authorities did all they could to ensure its efficient distribution to even the furthest-flung outpost.

Last but by no means least, most platoons enjoyed particularly cordial relations with their medical corpsman (or paramedic), who lived with them all the time and gave them a special type of reassurance that could come from no other source. The military memoirs from the Vietnam War seem to be pretty unanimous that their own local corpsman was personally devoted to the good health and welfare of everyone in the platoon, and selflessly unsparing in the efforts he would devote to them if they were wounded. And behind the corpsman there was always the "Dustoff" medevac helicopter, which represented the ultimate reassurance that any wounded soldier would quickly be returned to "The World."

Aftermath

Assuming a firebase was not captured by the enemy, a moment would come when it reached the natural end of its useful life and had to be dismantled. This might be only a few days after it had been built, if it was designed to support only one specific operation; or it might be many weeks, months or even years later. Whenever the moment came, the complete firebase would have to be picked up and shipped out almost in its entirety. All fortifications had to be demolished, and all materials and munitions that might possibly be put to use by the enemy had to be removed. As the Australian Bill Houston told the author:

> Because we knew the enemy made use of any military equipment left behind, bases were scrupulously cleaned up when they were evacuated. Weapon pits and bunkers were filled in, sandbags recovered or burned, rubbish burned and buried; later it was policy to evacuate any rubbish that might be useful to the enemy (e.g. tin cans that could be filled with plastic explosive to make mines etc.) and so on. Given the climate and vegetation, most FSBs would have reverted to secondary jungle fairly quickly.

All this implied a major lifting operation by helicopter or road transport, as well as perhaps the only exercise in "tidying up" that the firebase (or "shanty town") might have experienced during its entire working life. At FSPB Coral a convoy of some 300 trucks was required to move out the equipment, as well as numerous heavy-lift helicopters, one of which managed to drop the artillery radar from its sling, smashing it to pieces. It was a nervous time for other reasons, and there were a number of minor panics. Troops were inadequately briefed that their artillery was disposing of its remaining ammunition by shooting it off at such a high rate of fire that many imagined a major combat crisis was in progress. The engineers were also deliberately setting off large explosions in key command bunkers, which had the effect of undermining the confidence of the remaining garrison, since the destruction of those bunkers by shelling would normally have represented a massive tactical catastrophe. During the evacuation phase of most firebases, however, almost all of the "normal" rules would be turned inside out. This process was particularly nerve-wracking for the rearguard party at "Coral," which had to stay behind overnight and defend the entire site with only a fraction of the rifle strength that would normally be considered necessary for the task.[13]

Pulling out of a firebase was a serious operation in its own right, which could be almost as complex and demanding as the original operation to reconnoiter, occupy and build the base in the first place. Everything would have to be very carefully planned and coordinated, including full security precautions, over-watching sentries, and heavy firepower on call. In the nine-day withdrawal of the 1st Cavalry (Airmobile) from the Cambodian incursion of June 1970 the requirements for evacuating each firebase were deemed to be so great that only one per day was attempted, thereby allowing a maximum concentration of air assets and lift capacity for each one. The whole operation went off in a smooth and orderly manner. By contrast the ARVN withdrawal from their incursion into Laos in March 1971 was considerably less well planned. In fact it was conducted under chaotic conditions, as the chain of command stubbornly failed to think ahead or cover for setbacks, and the enemy mounted an ever-escalating series of attacks. The straggling convoys provided vulnerable targets as they headed back

---

[13] McAulay, Lex *The Battle of Coral – Fire Support Bases Coral & Balmoral, May 1968*, pp. 311–14.

Modern war cemetery for 10,000 NVA at Troung Son (just south of the DMZ and north of Con Thien, Quang Tri province). This whole area was always fought over especially fiercely – most famously at Khe Sanh in 1968, but scarcely less so at Quang Tri in 1972. It was standard tactical policy for the VC and NVA to keep their battle dead out of Freeworld hands, which means that only a very small proportion of them could be retrieved after the war for formal burial in cemeteries of this type. (Ed Flint and Paul Harris)

over the border, on bad roads and with sagging confidence in the ability of their air support to face up to the unprecedented storm of enemy AAA fire. In these circumstances, which were widely reported as "almost a rout," it was simply not possible to retrieve the many tons of warlike stores that had been deposited to build up each of the 19 firebases during the initial insertion phase. Much of the material was simply abandoned to the enemy, who knew all too well how to convert it to good account. As an object lesson in how not to evacuate a string of firebases, this particular operation must stand supreme.

Even when the evacuation of a particular firebase went smoothly, there were often recriminations that it might have been abandoned too soon, or for ethereal "high command" reasons that were impossible to explain to the troops who had laboriously built it up, and who may then have exposed themselves to fire in their "home" there over a long period of time. Soldiers were often tempted to speculate that if the site was so easily disposable, then surely it might not have been worth fighting and dying for in the first place. The classic case is the Khe Sanh Combat Base itself, which had first been occupied as an airstrip in 1962 and had endured an epic three-month USMC siege during early 1968, only to be abandoned somewhat abruptly in June that same year. Yet Khe Sanh was an exceptionally high-profile and large-scale case that could not fail to attract public attention. Far more corrosive, perhaps, were the many smaller and less notorious examples of essentially the same thing, where firebases were built at high tempo as a particular offensive sweep developed, only to be evacuated a few days or weeks later, as the focus of operations moved elsewhere. To the troops on the ground such laborious exercises could seem to be particularly irritating and futile, even though the acid fact was that the US forces in Vietnam never had enough manpower to control the whole territory from a permanent network of interlocking firebases. A great deal of jinking and dodging from one place to another was unavoidable, however uncomfortable it may have been to the soldiers who had to do it. It is doubtless also true that very few soldiers in Vietnam ever became genuinely wedded to life in a foxhole, regardless of however familiar or "homey" it may have become to them. On the contrary, almost any evacuation of a firebase was seen as a very welcome opportunity to get back to a main base area, which could boast facilities for showers, laundry and all the other lesser pleasures of the flesh.

Even less palatable were the cases when the same site would subsequently have to be reoccupied in later operations. This happened most frequently when the enemy returned to an area that had earlier been cleared by a Freeworld sweep, and then evacuated. For example in the Que Son Valley (a.k.a. "Death Valley," or "Dragon Valley") the Marines made offensive sweeps which led to heavy fighting against the 2nd NVA Division in April, August and September 1967, during Tet 1969 and then again in August 1969. In each case key positions would be occupied only to be abandoned quite soon afterwards, which meant the whole process would just have to be repeated the next time round.

If we now step back a little from the tactical details of evacuating firebases, we may take a higher perspective and ask just what general lessons might be learned from "the firebase war" in Vietnam. A number of different answers might be offered. In the first place there can be no doubt that the Americans demonstrated just how strong a position could be made in a short space of time, even if its garrison was as small as a couple of hundred men. With correct integration of artillery, air and electronic support, almost any site could be made practically invulnerable to attack by light infantry, although somewhat less so to massed tank assaults. By 1973 there had been a definite step forward in the US "art of war," with helicopter mobility taking its place among a greatly enhanced suite of other munitions and tactics for the defense. Meanwhile the renewal of the art of attack was progressing much less quickly, since the firebases in Vietnam were rarely able to ensure total successes for the search and destroy operations launched from them.

Still more significant, perhaps, was the inability of firebases to exert any great influence on the counter-insurgency war, or the nation-building war for the "hearts and minds" of the Vietnamese people. Firebases were closed compounds designed to keep their garrisons separate and protected from the surrounding population – and in fact many of them were built in rough country where "free fire zones" could be set up precisely because there was no population living there at all. It was Gen Westmoreland's policy to leave counter-insurgency to the ARVN while reserving the other Freeworld forces for mainforce battles in the deserted frontier regions. Therefore the firebases were optimized for "big bang" battles rather than for subtle political or psychological action. This approach suited the American art of war as a whole – but it offered few solutions to the many subtle political situations into which US troops would find themselves deployed during the three decades after their withdrawal from Vietnam. In this perspective the tactical successes represented by firebases could be seen as something of a backwater or irrelevance. Thus we can today find many firebases dotted around the world that are highly reminiscent of the Vietnam prototypes – but we cannot find many signs of successful counter-insurgency or nation-building.

A crater thought to be from a 1,000 lb. bomb in the freefire zone between Con Thien and the DMZ. Note the surrounding rubber trees, which today cover much of the DMZ. (Ed Flint and Paul Harris)

The sites today

As we have seen, the end point for any firebase was supposed to be its total demolition and removal, so that absolutely nothing of significance would be left on the site. However, this "policing of the battlefield" would surely be done less meticulously in some cases than in others, so that we might hope to find certain sites in which quite a lot remained for the tourist or battlefield archaeologist to inspect.

Alas for such hopes, the Vietnamese themselves soon systematically stripped bare any firebase sites that were left with any recoverable material when its garrison withdrew. First the VC and NVA would sift through the ruins for anything that might be turned to military use. Unexploded shells, bombs or grenades might be turned into booby traps, while expended cartridge cases might be refilled and recycled. Damaged weapons might be lovingly handcrafted back into working order, and even discarded sandbags might be collected for future reuse. Then, following this initial "military" pillaging of the site, there would come a second, "civilian" phase.

It was a singularly unedifying feature of the Vietnam war that for over 20 years after the USA had lost it, she continued to maintain a vindictive economic blockade on the victors, who had already suffered over 10 times as many human casualties as the Americans themselves. The blockade had dire effects on the civilian population. An informed, recent visitor to the battlefields wrote to the author:

The situation for ordinary folk in Vietnam 1975–85 was utterly desperate. It is not clear whether many people actually starved but the poverty was extreme … About the only way that people could get their hands on ready cash was to get scrap metal. Most of the casualties to civilians from munitions at this period were not (as is widely supposed in the West) innocent farmers running their ploughs over bombs, but people deliberately going looking for the stuff and in many cases physically pulling it apart. So desperate were folk that they pulled apart concrete firebases with the most elementary tools (or bare hands) just to get at the metal reinforcing rods inside the concrete. Thus almost nothing remains of most of these places except trenches, fox holes, the remains of sandbags and sometimes the plastic casing for LAW 66mm rockets and claymore mines – which evidently have no financial value. The only metal we saw was a few M16 bullets and a few pellets from Claymores. There must have been so many countless millions of these that a few were missed … One problem with (visiting) the bases is that you have to be careful to distinguish holes dug for military purposes in the sixties and early seventies from holes dug to look for metal in the late seventies and eighties especially – though the scrap metal hunt is still going on. Little effort is being made to preserve most of these places and coffee and rubber (amongst other things) is, in many cases, being planted over them. This radically alters the appearance that they once had. It is now very difficult to see from Con Thien (for example) the sorts of vistas it once commanded.

Michael P. Kelley also wrote:[14]

The Vietnamese have virtually erased every trace of what they call the "American War". And whatever the Vietnamese might have overlooked, the jungle, monsoons and soil erosion have erased for them … When the Americans left in 1973, those

---

[14] Kelley, Michael P. *Where We Were in Vietnam. A comprehensive guide to the firebases, military installations and naval vessels of the Vietnam war 1945–75*, p. xvii

What remains of the 173d Airborne Brigade's and 4th Division's main base and airfield "Dak To 2" (Kontum Province). Today the site is being used to dry manioc. Through most of 1967 it was at the center of a fierce and prolonged campaign, which ended in a massive explosion of an ammo dump in the base in November. It was rebuilt in December of that year. (Ed Flint and Paul Harris)

bases not taken by the ARVN often disappeared practically overnight; dismantled by nearby villagers intent on improving their homes or in marketing the material.

He added that as well as a pressing economic motive for this removal, there was also a political desire to wipe out any symbols of the French or American colonial occupation.

In short, the prospect is not good for any modern student who wishes to inspect the sites of 1965–75 firebases. Vietnam itself is now open and welcoming to tourists, and its basic topography is largely unchanged. The "Rockpile," for example, still stands as a craggy height commanding wide views towards Khe Sanh to the west and the coastal plain to the east. Many disused airstrips may still be seen, although their asphalt surfaces and other amenities will long since have been removed by either the Americans or the Vietnamese. But if the visitor wishes to search further into the precise layout of the fortifications at any given site, he will find he faces a very frustrating task. Some overgrown berms and ambiguous holes in the ground may be detected, as well as the occasional lump of concrete which had perhaps started life as the hard standing for a long-vanished mess hall, or maybe as part of what is now a badly damaged pillbox. In general, however, far too much material has now been removed for any coherent picture to emerge from the little that remains, so that it would today take a highly determined and well-informed team of specialist archaeologists to achieve any better results. This should not perhaps surprise us very much, since in every other war in history the fieldworks have tended to disappear far faster than the permanent fortifications. Indeed, in Vietnam itself the early 19th century bastioned fortress of Hué is still standing (more or less) proud after 200 years, despite some very heavy bombardments in 1968; whereas the much more modern and potent – but temporary – firebases have all but totally disappeared after just 40 years. But even then, in Vietnam the spectacularly energetic determination of both sides to strip so many thousands of firebases so bare within such little time does force us to ask whether this represents some sort of international record.

However reluctantly, we now have to accept that the best way to visualize what existed during the war is not by inspecting the ground at all, but by referring back to the written and photo-graphic records made at the time. Admittedly there are still many museums and monuments that may be visited in modern Vietnam, mainly set up to commemorate the people's long sacrifice and eventual victory. These will often have interesting items of equipment or weaponry on display; but they will not really take our understanding of the firebases very much further forward than that. Indeed, something similar may also be said of those military museums that can occasionally be found in the USA, Australia or their other wartime allied states, which bother to mention Vietnam at all. Since this war was in the end a Freeworld defeat, we cannot expect a great effort of interpretation to be directed towards the general public, even though some thousands of very excellent specialist books are available – a very few of which are listed in the bibliographical section that follows.

61

Select bibliography

Hay, J.H. *Tactical and Material Innovations* (Vietnam Studies series, Department of the Army, Washington, DC, 1974). One of a number of technical reports in this excellent series.

Herr, Michael *Dispatches* (first published 1977; Picador edition, London 1978). Everything anyone needs for the "surreal" side of the Vietnam War, as seen by a journalist.

Kelley, Michael P. *Where We Were in Vietnam. A comprehensive guide to the firebases, military installations and naval vessels of the Vietnam War 1945–75* (Hellgate Press, Central Point, Oregon 2002). Not just "comprehensive," but gigantic! A truly invaluable mine of information, not only for its listing of firebases and LZs but also for its glossary and many other details.

McAulay, Lex *The Battle of Coral – Fire Support Bases Coral & Balmoral, May 1968* (Hutchinson Australia, 1988). Detailed tactical and human account of two Australian firebases that had to beat off some major attacks during their three weeks' existence.

McCauley, Greg *Buckle For Your Dust: Miniature Wargames in Vietnam 1965–73* (Paddy Griffith Associates, Nuneaton, 1995). Includes details of weapons and troop types.

Marshall, S.L.A. *Bird, the Chistmastide Battle* (New York, 1968). The most dramatic firebase battle described by this veteran military journalist; all his other books on the Vietnam War are also well worth study.

Moore, Harold G. and Galloway, Joseph L. *We Were Soldiers Once … and Young* (HarperCollins, New York, 1992). Stirring detailed account of the Ia Drang battle at LZs X-Ray and Albany.

Nicoli, Robert J. *Fire Support Base Development*. Written during a second tour in I Corps area, 1969; now on the internet at http://members.aol.com/warlibrary/vwfsb.htm.

Ott, David Ewing *Field Artillery, 1954–73* (Vietnam Studies series, Department of the Army, Washington, DC, 1975). Essential reading for the "fire" part of any "firebase."

Ploger, R.R. *US Army Engineers, 1965–70* (Vietnam Studies series, Department of the Army, Washington, DC, 1974). Building the "base" part of any "firebase."

Rottman, Gordon L. *Khe Sanh 1967–68: Marines Battle for Vietnam's Vital Hilltop Base* (Campaign No. 150, Osprey Publishing, Oxford, 2005). A full account of the battle.

Rottman, Gordon L. *Special Forces Camps in Vietnam 1961–70* (Fortress No. 33, Osprey Publishing, Oxford, 2005). An excellent and very detailed listing of all the small considerations (from the dimensions of timber to the penetration of rockets against concrete) that went into the building of a Special Forces camp.

Starry, D.A. *Mounted Combat in Vietnam* (Vietnam Studies series, Department of the Army, Washington, DC, 1978). An insight into how armor was neglected early in the US deployment, but used increasingly after 1967.

Tolson, J.J. *Airmobility, 1961–71* (Vietnam Studies series, Department of the Army, Washington, DC, 1973). Excellent technical study of the birth and development of helicopter operations.

Rapid fire from an M102 105mm howitzer at FSB Charlie II (Quang Tri province) during Operation *Dewey Canyon*, March 26, 1971. Note the role of the single-unit trail in supporting the gun while the wheels are raised. The gunners are from Battery C, 6th Bn, 11th Artillery. (US National Archives)

Glossary and abbreviations

ACAV Armored cavalry assault vehicle – an up-gunned and up-armored APC.

ADSID Air-delivered seismic intrusion detectors (unmanned sensor).

APC Armored personnel carrier – almost always an M113.

ARA Aerial rocket artillery – rocket-firing helicopters operated in batteries according to artillery procedures.

ARVN Army of the Republic of Vietnam – the pro-Freeworld South Vietnamese regular army.

ATF Australian Task Force.

Bn Battalion.

CIDG Civilian irregular defense group – local militias organized by USSF.

CMP Corrugated metal pipe.

CONEX Container express – a heavy steel container for shipping heavy freight, which could be loaded onto trucks, trains, ships – or even Sky Cranes.

CP Command post.

CTZ Corps tactical zone. They were numbered from I to IV reading from north to south in South Vietnam. The US Marine Corps provided much of the manpower in I Corps, while the Army manned the other three.

DMZ The demilitarized zone, adjacent to the border between North and South Vietnam: the scene of much of the heaviest fighting.

FAC Forward air controller.

FDC Fire direction center – the center of decision-making for outgoing fire from a firebase.

FFSB Forward fire support base.

FOB Forward operating base – a major fixed base or combat base.

Freeworld forces An extraordinarily disparate coalition of convenience which, with widely varying motives and degrees of enthusiasm, was attempting to support the extraordinarily unpredictable and unreliable South Vietnamese government and ARVN. Until 1973 it was led and largely bankrolled by the USA, and at its peak it included South Korea, Thailand, the Philippines, Australia and New Zealand.

FSB Fire support base – a pretty permanent position.

FSCC Fire support co-ordination center.

FSPB Fire support patrol base – for one operation.

H&I Harassment and interdiction fire.

Laterite Gravel made of fragments of compacted red-brown clay.

LAW M-72 light antitank weapon, to fire a 62mm shaped charge up to 600m.

LZ Landing zone: anywhere used to land helicopters.

MACV Military Assistance Command, Vietnam.

NDP Night defensive position.

NOD Night observation device (first deployed in 1968).

NVA North Vietnamese Army – the communist forces attempting to reunify Vietnam.

PSP Pierced steel planks.

PX Post exchange – where the soldiers could buy familiar American goods (e.g. foods, cigarettes, magazines etc.) in foreign lands.

RPG Rocket-propelled grenade. Originally designed as a handheld (shaped charge) antitank weapon, it was widely and effectively used by communist forces in Vietnam against fortifications and personnel. Ironically it was relatively ineffective against APCs and even tanks.

SLAR Side-looking airborne radar.

SP Self-propelled. The US inventory included SP versions of all their artillery pieces; but towed versions of the 105mm and 155mm howitzers were preferred because they could be carried by helicopters.

TOC Tactical operations center.

USMC United States Marine Corps.

USSF US Special Forces.

VC As in "Victor Charlie," according to the military alphabet, hence often simply "Charlie" – the Viet Cong. The pro-freedom and pro-reunification South Vietnamese irregular army.

A sandbagged ammunition bunker at FSB Conquer/Conquest (in Cambodia), with a cleared gun position behind (Battery A, 2d Bn, 9th Artillery, II Field Force). Apart from the sandbags themselves, most of the elements in the construction appear to have been scrounged or adapted from other purposes. The flag demonstrates the omnipresence of Texas. (US National Archives)

Index

References to illustrations are shown in **bold**.